Prank University

Prank University

THE ULTIMATE GUIDE TO COLLEGE'S GREATEST TRADITION

JOHN AUSTIN

THREE RIVERS PRESS New York

PUBLISHED IN THE UNITED STATES BY THREE RIVERS PRESS, AN IMPRINT OF THE CROWN PUBLISHING GROUP, A DIVISION OF RANDOM HOUSE, INC., NEW YORK.
WWW.CROWNPUBLISHING.COM

LIBRARY OF CONGRESS CATALOGING-IN-PUBLICATION DATA

AUSTIN, JOHN, 1978–
PRANK UNIVERSITY: THE ULTIMATE GUIDE TO COLLEGE'S GREATEST TRADITION/ JOHN AUSTIN.
1. PRACTICAL JOKES. I. TITLE.
PN6231.P67A98 2006
817'.02—DC22 200603152

ISBN-13: 978-0-307-33843-3
ISBN-10: 0-307-33843-6

PRINTED IN THE UNITED STATES OF AMERICA

DESIGN BY JOHN AUSTIN

10 9 8 7 6 5 4 3 2 1

FIRST EDITION

LONG LIVE THE DEAD MONKEYS & JIGGLE PIGS

ACKNOWLEDGMENTS

I WOULD FIRST LIKE TO THANK MY EXTRAORDINARY AGENT, LAURIE ABKEMEIER, WHOSE BRILLIANT GUIDANCE AND HARD WORK MADE THIS BOOK A SUCCESS; MY COLLEGE ROOMMATES, FOR PUTTING UP WITH MY SHENANIGANS AND NOT KILLING ME; ALL OF FIRST-FLOOR JETER HALL; D-BO; DERRICK BASLER; LEE CAMINITI; JON DUKERSCHEIN; JASON HEIBERGER; MARC FECHTNER; RYAN HINTZ; JANEL HOEKENGA; JON PFEFFER; JEFF JAEGER; JOHN JONES; MIKE KLEINHANS; BILL MILLER; MIKE LEIGHTON; AARON MARX; SCOTT MEYER; N8; CARRIE PASKO; SARA SEYMOUR; RAMBO; NICK THE PRICK AND TIM SCHOMMER, FOR ALWAYS HITTING ME HARDER THAN I HIT THEM; MY MOM, FOR ALL THE TALENT, AND MY DAD, FOR THE ENTREPRENEURIAL SPIRIT; MY BROTHER, TOM, FOR SHARING A ROOM WITH ME; MY SISTER, JESS, FOR NOT ASSASSINATING ME; CARRIE THORNTON AND EVERYONE AT THREE RIVERS PRESS; AND, OF COURSE, MY BEAUTIFUL AND UNDERSTANDING WIFE, SARA.

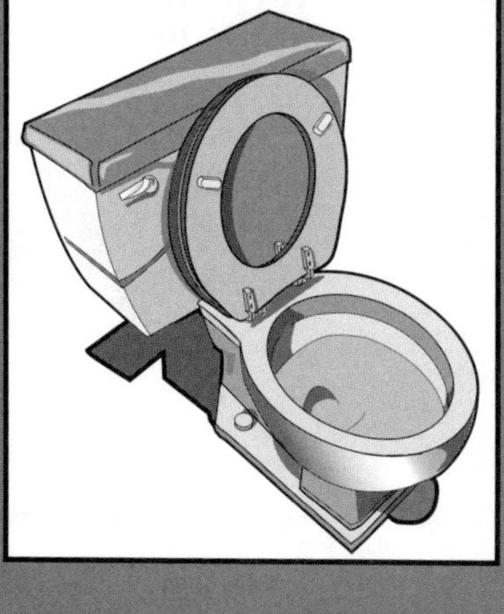

CONTENTS

Prank

UNIVERSITY

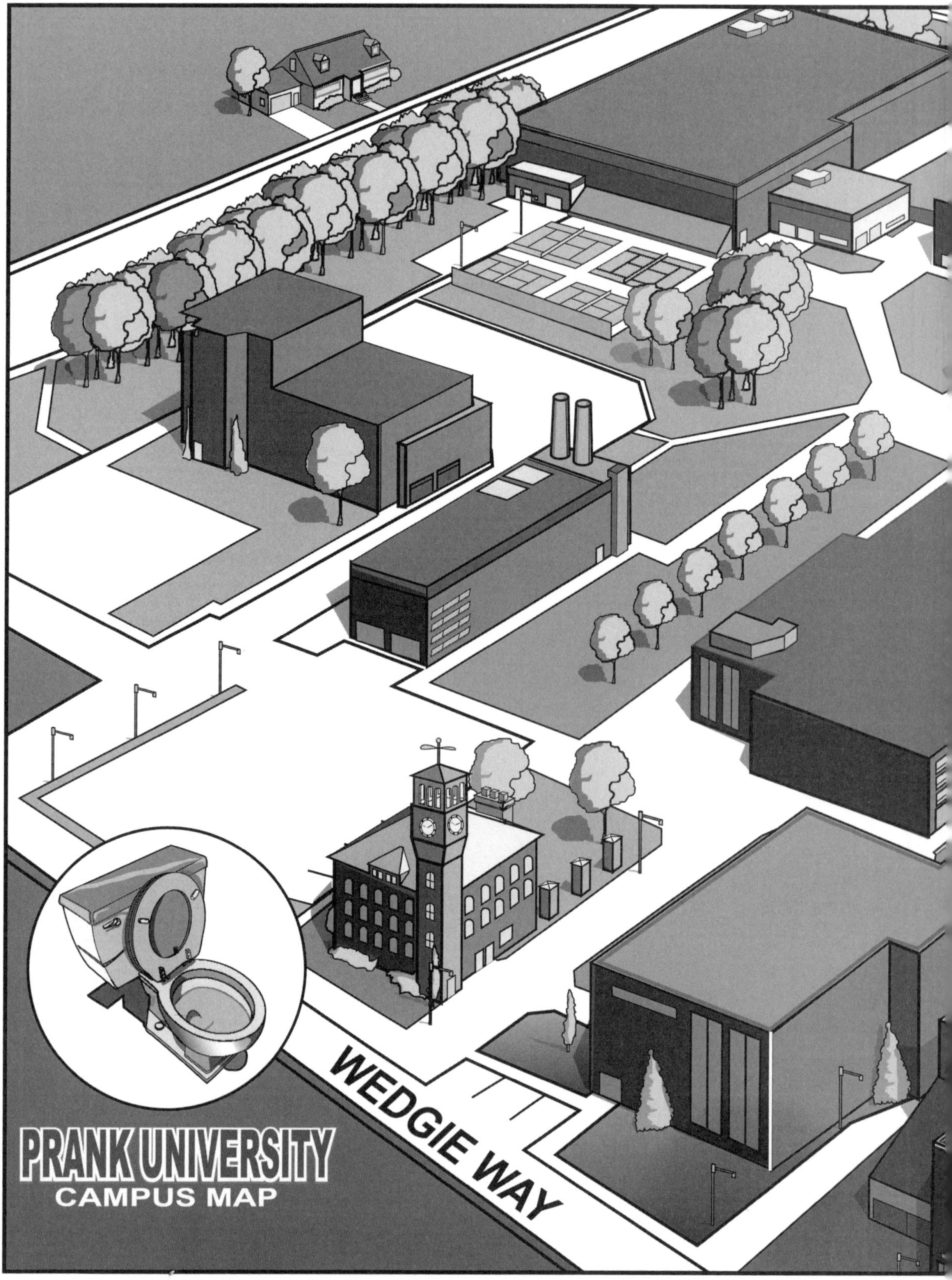
WEDGIE WAY
PRANK UNIVERSITY
CAMPUS MAP

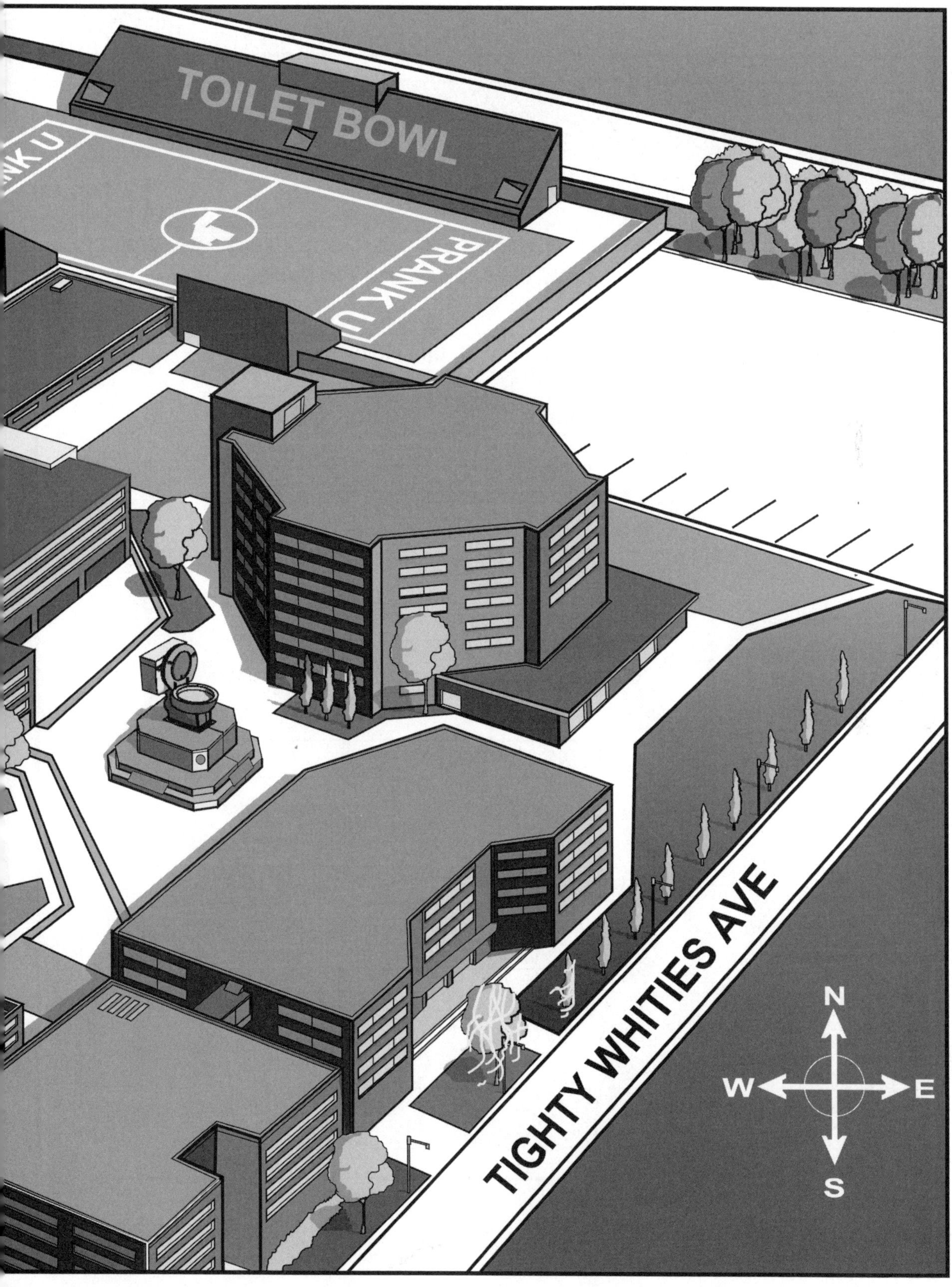
TOILET BOWL
PRANK U
NK U
TIGHTY WHITIES AVE
N
W
E
S

ICONS

How to read and use this book:

ICONS

- ADDED BONUS INCLUDED
- THIS IS TOO GOOD NOT TO FILM
- SHOULD BE DONE DURING THE DAY
- SHOULD BE DONE DURING THE NIGHT
- COSTS MONEY
- DOESN'T COST A CENT
- FINE OR TIME
- NUMBER OF PEOPLE NEEDED
- OFF-CAMPUS
- DIFFICULTY OF PRANK

SIMPLE ←→ DIFFICULT

1 2 3 4 5

INTRODUCTION

WELCOME TO *PRANK UNIVERSITY*. CLASS IS IN SESSION! THIS BOOK IS A FULLY ILLUSTRATED GUIDE ON HOW TO EXECUTE ONE HUNDRED TOP-RATED PRANKS. *PU* OFFERS A COMPILATION OF EASY-TO-PULL-OFF STUNTS THAT ANY BORED OR MISCHIEVOUS STUDENT—OR ANY OVERGROWN PRANKSTER—WILL LOVE. THIS BOOK IS A TOOL TO FUEL YOUR IMAGINATION AND TO EVEN THE ODDS AGAINST AN EVER BIGGER AND DUMBER OPPONENT. SIMPLY PERUSE THE PAGES OF THIS BEAUTIFULLY CRAFTED BOOK AND YOU'LL CERTAINLY FIND MORE THAN A FEW NEW CHUCKLES. BEST OF ALL, THESE INGENIOUS PRANKS HAVE LIFE BEYOND THE CAMPUS AND CAN BE EASILY ORCHESTRATED AGAINST ANNOYING COLLEAGUES, DEADBEAT ROOMMATES, AND PESKY IN-LAWS WHO HAVE OVERSTAYED THEIR WELCOME. JOHN AUSTIN, FOUNDER OF THE PRANK UNIVERSITY, ATTENDED COLLEGE FOR FIVE YEARS, AND DURING THAT TIME HE PUSHED HIS ROOMMATES TO THE EDGE WITH ONE INGENIOUS PRANK AFTER ANOTHER. HE LIVED BY THE MOTTO "WHY SHOW COMPASSION TO YOUR ROOMMATES WHEN YOU CAN TERRORIZE THEM TO THE POINT OF INSANITY?" ENJOY!

PRANK UNIVERSITY

001 BAG OF POO

0 1 6

SUCCESSFUL ATTEMPTS																
1	2	3	4	5	6	7	8	9	10	11	12	13	14	15	16	17

POOP IS ONE OF MAN'S EARLIEST CREATIONS AND STILL PLAYS AN IMPORTANT ROLE IN TODAY'S SOCIETY. THE FIRST PAPER BAG–MAKING MACHINE WAS INVENTED IN THE 1960s. THIS PRANK BRINGS THESE TWO ITEMS—POOP AND THE PAPER BAG—TOGETHER IN AN EXCITING SYMBIOTIC RELATIONSHIP, ESPECIALLY WHEN THEY MEET ON A FRONT PORCH. YOUR FATHER HAS PROBABLY SHARED SOME OF HIS ADOLESCENT PRANKS WITH YOU; MOST LIKELY THIS WAS ONE OF THEM.

FILL A PAPER BAG WITH POOP FROM ANY SOURCE, PUT IT ON SOMEONE'S PORCH, THEN LIGHT IT, RING THE DOORBELL, AND RUN LIKE HELL! IT IS ESSENTIAL THAT YOU ARE NOT SEEN. THE RESIDENT WILL START TO STOMP OUT THE FIRE, BUT (UN)FORTUNATELY, HIS SHOES WILL BE COVERED WITH YOUR DIRTY DEED!

ADDED BONUS: After the resident opens the front door, run to the back door and ring the doorbell. He'll hightail it to the back door, tracking poop through his house.

PRANK UNIVERSITY

002 TOOTHPASTE TICKLE

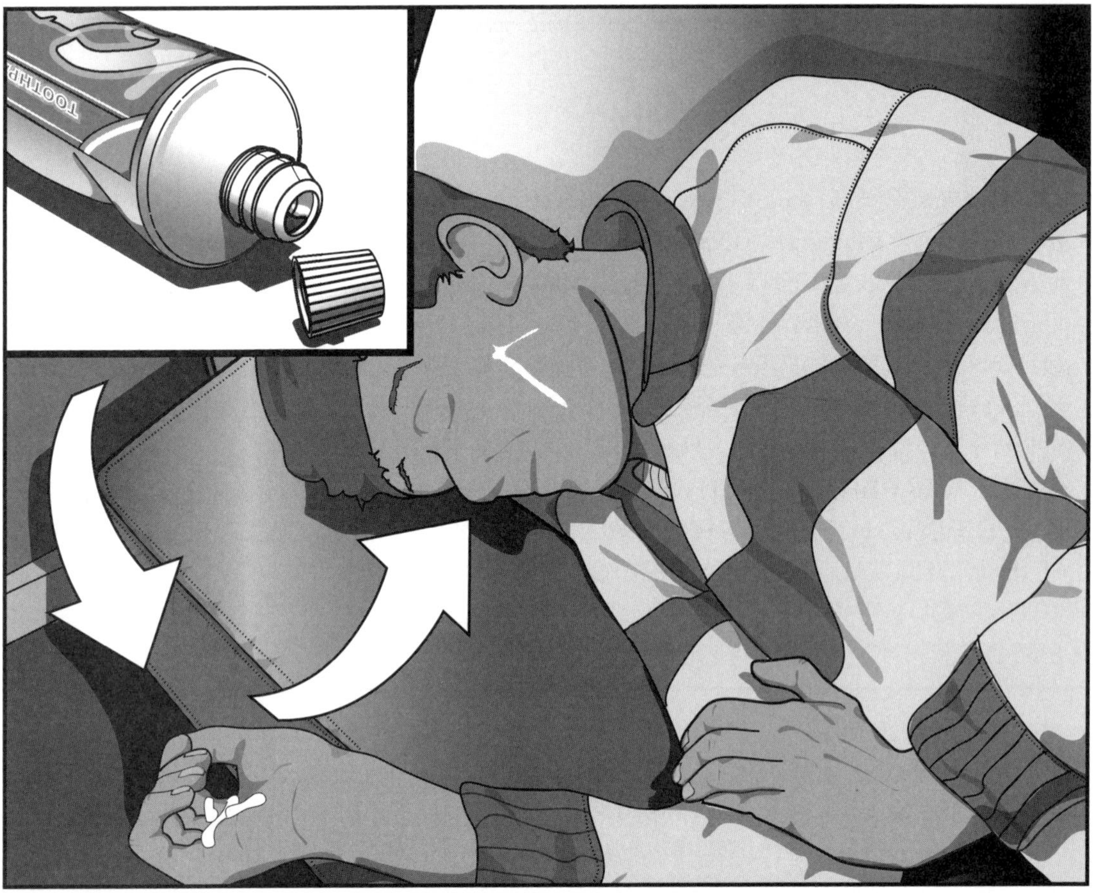

2

SUCCESSFUL ATTEMPTS

1	2	3	4	5	6	7	8	9	10	11	12	13	14	15	16	17

WITH MEMORIES OF YOUR CHILDHOOD SLEEPOVERS DANCING IN YOUR HEAD, YOU STRUGGLE TO CONTAIN YOUR GLEE AS YOU FILL THE PALM OF YOUR SLEEPING VICTIM'S HAND WITH TOOTHPASTE. FIGHTING BACK THE LAUGHTER, YOU LEAN IN TO TICKLE THE NOSE, AND THEN IT HAPPENS—THE HAND QUICKLY GOES TO THE FACE, TRYING TO RESOLVE THE MYSTERIOUS ITCH. THE HAND THEN STARTS SPREADING THE PASTE OVER THE MOUTH AND INTO THE DROOL. NEXT, THE PASTE MAKES ITS WAY INTO THE HAIR AND DOWN OVER THE EAR. CONGRATULATIONS! TONIGHT YOU FOUND VENGEANCE FOR HIS HOOKING YOU UP WITH THAT "BUTT-HER-FACE" LAST NIGHT.

ADDED BONUS: If you're running low on toothpaste, anything in your refrigerator will work: honey, ketchup, mustard, mayo, sour cream, butter, even whipped cream. Hot sauce is not advised, unless it's truly deserved.

PRANK UNIVERSITY

003 RAIN MÂCHÉ

									SUCCESSFUL ATTEMPTS							
1	2	3	4	5	6	7	8	9	10	11	12	13	14	15	16	17

IT'S RAINING, IT'S POURING, AND YOUR HALLMATES ARE SNORING! AS YOU MAKE YOUR WAY HOME FROM THE BARS, PASSING UNSAVORY TYPES AND OTHER DRUNKARDS, COLLECT FREE NEWSPAPERS. APRIL SHOWERS HAVE BROUGHT OPPORTUNITY ON THIS LONELY NIGHT; BE RESOURCEFUL. I HAVE CONFIDENCE IN YOU. PERHAPS YOU'VE NEVER REALIZED IT, BUT THERE ARE EVEN A LOT OF NEWSPAPERS ON PEOPLE'S PORCHES. HELP YOURSELF! SOAK THE PAPERS IN PUDDLES ALONG THE CURB, OPEN THEM UP TO ACHIEVE THEIR FULL SQUARE FOOTAGE, AND THEN PLACE THEM ON YOUR VICTIM'S VEHICLE. YOU CAN COVER A CAR FAIRLY QUICKLY WITH THE HELP OF OTHERS.

ADDED BONUS: Household toilet paper can be substituted for newspaper. The real kick in the balls is when the sun rises the next morning.

PRANK UNIVERSITY

004 LAXATIVE SPECIAL

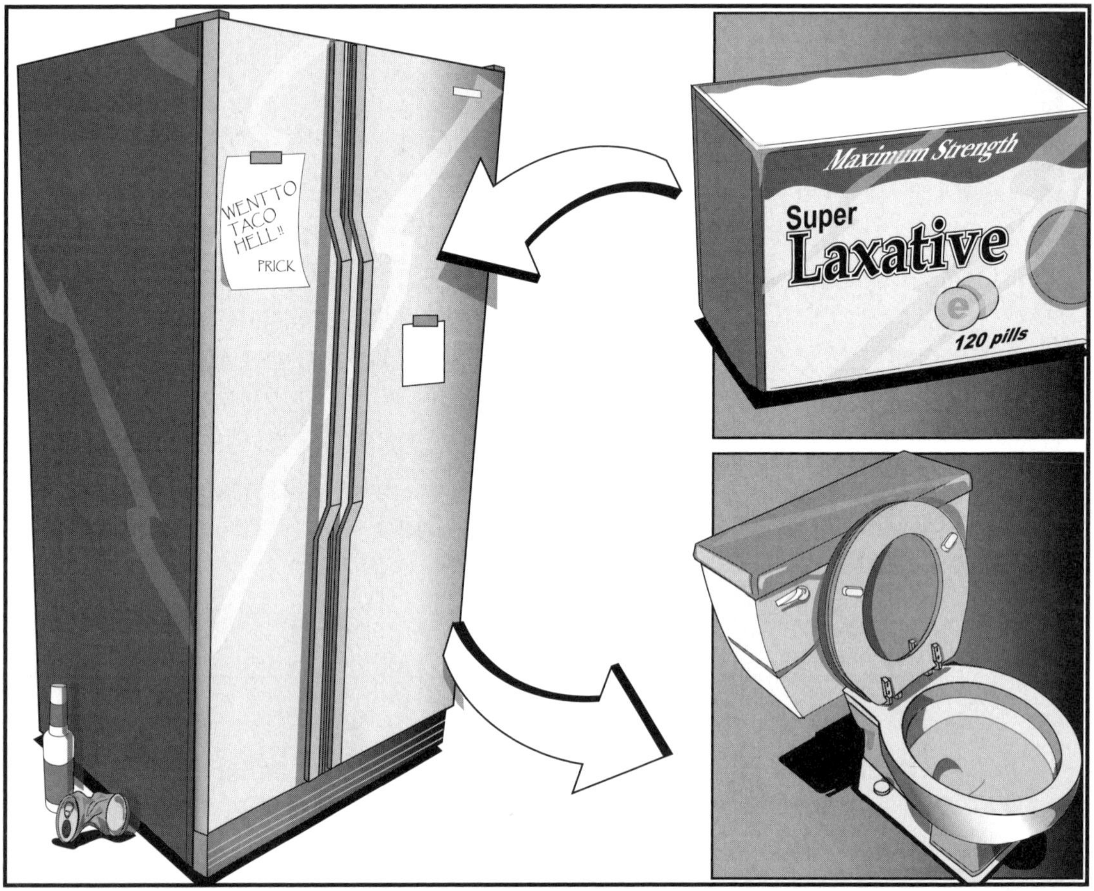

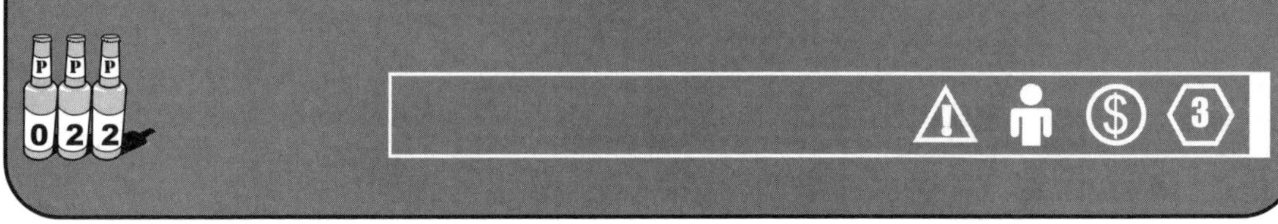

SUCCESSFUL ATTEMPTS

1	2	3	4	5	6	7	8	9	10	11	12	13	14	15	16	17

STIMULANT LAXATIVES HAVE ONE VERY PLEASANT USE: SCARING THE CRAP OUT OF YOUR ROOMMATES. SOME ROOMMATES JUST DON'T GRASP THE CONCEPT OF NOT EATING OTHER PEOPLE'S FOOD. IF THIS IS A PROBLEM IN YOUR HOUSEHOLD, PURCHASE SOMETHING THAT LOOKS ABSOLUTELY SCRUMPTIOUS, LIKE BROWNIES OR POWDERED-SUGAR DONUTS. CONCEAL THE LAXATIVE TABLETS IN THE TREATS. OFFER SOME TO YOUR FRIENDS, TELLING THEM HOW GOOD THEY ARE. SIT BACK AND WAIT.

ADDED BONUS: After serving up the "Laxative Special," hide all the toilet paper in the house. Just don't forget where you hid it, fool!

PRANK UNIVERSITY

005 CRUCIFIXION

024

SUCCESSFUL ATTEMPTS

1	2	3	4	5	6	7	8	9	10	11	12	13	14	15	16	17

MUTED LAUGHTER CAN BE HEARD AS NEIGHBORS APPROACH THE HALF-NAKED VICTIM. HIS UNCONSCIOUS BODY, A PRIME TARGET FOR A DUCT-TAPE CRUCIFIXION, RESTS QUIETLY. YOU ARE ONLY FULFILLING YOUR SWORN OBLIGATION TO AGGRAVATE THE FIRST POOR SOUL TO PASS OUT. BEGIN WORK ON HIS FEET AND WAIST, TO IMMOBILIZE HIM. AFTER THAT, GATHER HALF A DOZEN FRIENDS TO HOIST THE VICTIM SLOWLY AGAINST THE DORM WALL, AND THEN FINISH UP WITH HIS ARMS. AWAKE AND EXHAUSTED, HE NO LONGER STRUGGLES. HE HAS BECOME A TOURIST ATTRACTION, AS DISTURBED BUT BEAUTIFUL GIRLS BEGIN TAKING PHOTOS WITH HIM.

ADDED BONUS: If you don't have the manpower to pull this off, tape him to his bed by wrapping the tape around the bed frame.

PRANK UNIVERSITY

006 DRUNKEN PUKE

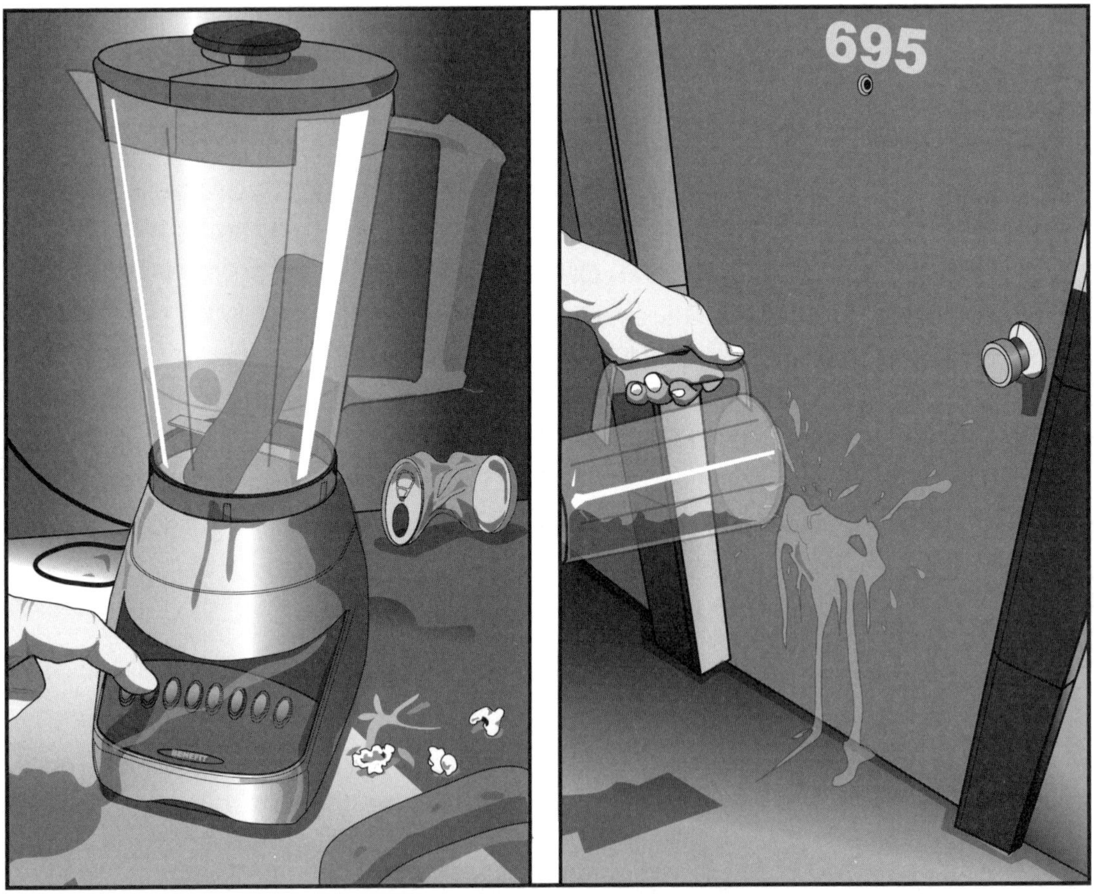

SUCCESSFUL ATTEMPTS

1	2	3	4	5	6	7	8	9	10	11	12	13	14	15	16	17

CAN YOU IMAGINE WAKING UP SATURDAY MORNING AND FINDING OUT SOMEONE HAD THE AUDACITY TO VOMIT, BARF, CACK, PUKE, BLOW CHUNKS, SPEW, UPCHUCK, AND CASCADE ON YOUR DOOR? THIS RECIPE CALLS FOR ANY AND ALL INGREDIENTS. IN ORDER TO PULL OFF THIS PRANK, YOU WILL HAVE TO BLEND A REALISTIC COMBINATION TO ACHIEVE AUTHENTIC-LOOKING PUKE. THAT SAID, MODEST PROPORTIONS ARE BELIEVABLE, SO NO TWENTY–HOT DOG REGURGITATION IS NECESSARY. JUST REMEMBER THAT IF YOUR FLOOR'S RESIDENTIAL ADVISOR (R.A.) CATCHES YOU, YOU WILL HAVE TO CLEAN UP THIS MONSTROSITY. ALSO, MAKE SURE YOU PROPEL THE MIX AGAINST THE DOOR TO CREATE THE ILLUSION OF A TRUE HEAVE.

ADDED BONUS: Squirt some fake blood on the door and doorknob to create the illusion that someone was trying to get into the room.

PRANK UNIVERSITY

007 LINCOLN LOCK

SUCCESSFUL ATTEMPTS

1	2	3	4	5	6	7	8	9	10	11	12	13	14	15	16	17

LIKE YOUR FATHER, AND HIS FATHER BEFORE HIM, GENERATIONS OF PRANKSTERS HAVE PASSED DOWN THE LINCOLN LOCK; NOW IT'S YOUR TURN. AFTER YOUR NEXT-DOOR NEIGHBOR GOES INTO HIS ROOM FOR THE NIGHT, FIND FOUR PENNIES. YOU'LL NEED ONE PERSON TO PUSH THE DOOR IN AS HARD AS HE CAN, AND SOMEONE ELSE TO STACK THE PENNIES ON TOP OF ONE ANOTHER AND SLIDE THEM IN BETWEEN THE DOOR AND THE FRAME. BY DOING THIS, YOU PUT ENOUGH PRESSURE ON THE LOCK THAT IT CAN'T BE OPENED. BEWARE: RESIDENTIAL ADVISORS HATE THIS BECAUSE USUALLY THEY ARE CALLED FOR THE UNLOCKING OF THE LINCOLN LOCK. ALSO, THIS PRANK COULD RESULT IN A FINE—IT'S A FIRE HAZARD!

ADDED BONUS: This prank only costs four cents, so if you did this once a day for one hundred days, it would only cost you four dollars!

PRANK UNIVERSITY

008 HOUSE FOR SALE

SUCCESSFUL ATTEMPTS

1	2	3	4	5	6	7	8	9	10	11	12	13	14	15	16	17

IT'S AMAZING HOW MANY "FOR SALE" AND "FOR RENT" SIGNS YOU CAN FIND WHEN YOU'RE LOOKING FOR THEM. YOUR TOWN IS PROBABLY LITTERED WITH THEM. DO YOUR COMMUNITY A FAVOR AND HELP CLEAN THEM UP. THIS ONE WILL BE A TWO-MAN JOB; YOU'LL NEED A GOOD DRIVER AND A FAST RUNNER. TAKE A DRIVE AND COLLECT AS MANY OF THESE SIGNS AS YOU CAN WITHIN AN HOUR. DRIVE TO A FRIEND'S HOUSE AND PLACE THESE SIGNS IN HIS FRONT YARD. BE SURE TO WATCH OUT FOR THE POLICE.

ADDED BONUS: Even better, make every house on that street for sale except your friend's house!

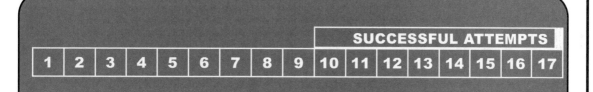

PRANK UNIVERSITY

009 PERSONAL AD

I AM A 59-year-old,
I am interested in a Female who
romantic, to enjoy time together by
building up friendship first... Later
romance and beyond. Please call
#4022
FUN-LOVING EXPERIMENTAL!
26 year-old, 5'10" White Male.
Seeking Gentleman to spend time
with. Enjoy social drinking,
gambling, and Rambo movies.
Friendship, possibly more. Please
Contact me....take me away!!
#4112
SPRING INTO MY LIFE! 26 year-
old, 6'2" Single White Male. Tri-
athlon competitor who enjoys the
Graphic arts! Give me a call and
I'll pick you up in the Beretta GT!
PROFESSIONAL
#3321
#4032
#4321

3

									SUCCESSFUL ATTEMPTS							
1	2	3	4	5	6	7	8	9	10	11	12	13	14	15	16	17

IF ONE OF YOUR ROOMMATES IS HAVING TROUBLE FINDING LOVE, HERE IS A SOLUTION. A FEW YEARS AGO, YOU WOULD HAVE HAD TO TRAVEL DOWN TO THE NEWSPAPER HEADQUARTERS AND HANDWRITE AN AD FOR THE NEXT WEEK'S PAPER. BUT TIMES HAVE CHANGED—NOW YOU CAN PLACE A PERSONAL AD FROM THE COMFORT OF YOUR OWN HOME, WITH YOUR COMPUTER. RUN A TWO-WEEK AD IN THE LOCAL "ALTERNATIVE" SECTION FOR YOUR FRIEND, BUT DON'T LET HIM IN ON THE JOKE. FOR TWO WEEKS HE'LL BE GETTING ALL TYPES OF WEIRD PHONE CALLS ON HIS CELL PHONE. IT WILL BE VERY AMUSING WATCHING HIM EXPLAIN TO HIS GIRLFRIEND THAT HE HAS NO IDEA WHY THESE MEN KEEP CALLING HIM.

ADDED BONUS: You can also put an ad in the paper looking for "hot women, needed for onetime photo shoot, generous pay." List your friend's phone number.

PRANK UNIVERSITY

010 PLASTIC FANTASTIC

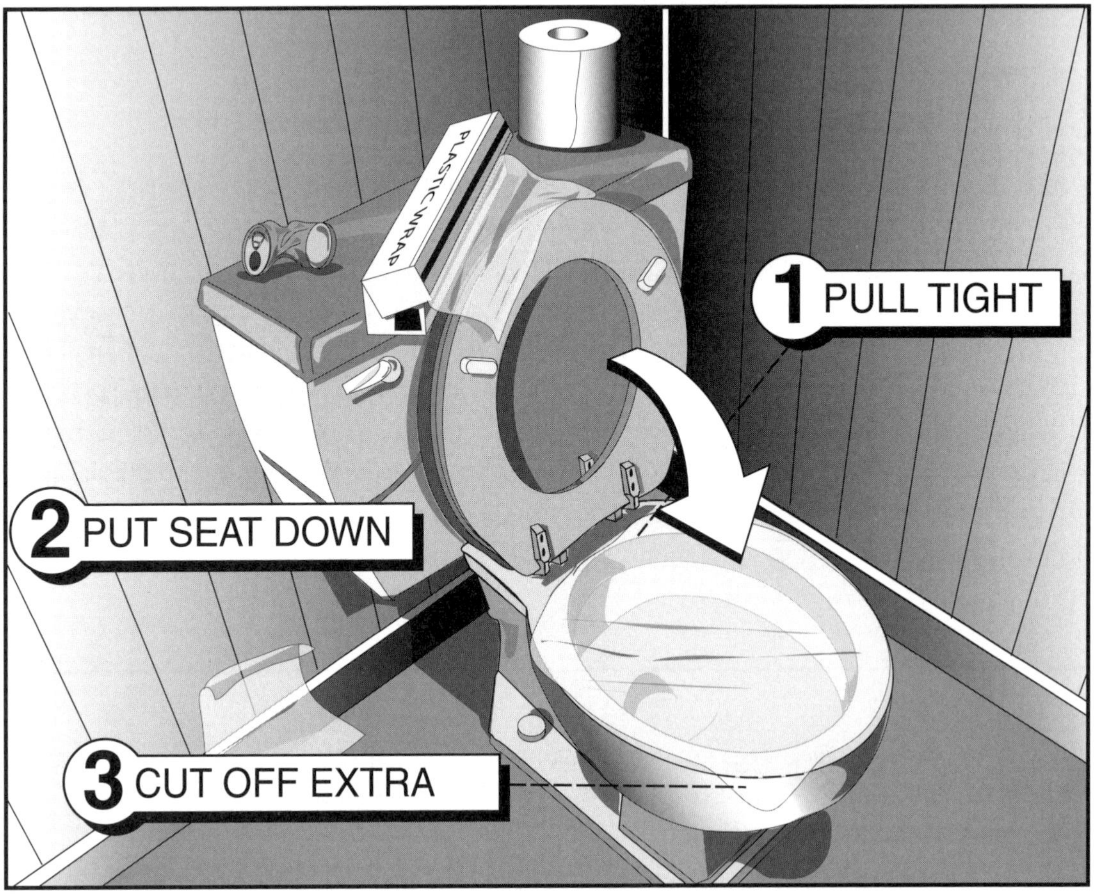

									SUCCESSFUL ATTEMPTS							
1	2	3	4	5	6	7	8	9	10	11	12	13	14	15	16	17

THIS PRANK PROBABLY WORKS BEST IN A DORMITORY. THAT'S BECAUSE MOST ON-CAMPUS STUDENTS USE THE PUBLIC TOILET FOR ONLY TWO THINGS: PUKING AND POOPING, AND SOMETIMES BOTH AT THE SAME TIME.

STRETCH A SHEET OF PLASTIC WRAP TIGHT OVER THE TOILET BOWL, AND THEN CUT OFF ANY EXTRA, OR JUST HIDE IT UNDER THE SEAT. YOUR VICTIM WILL ENTER THE STALL LOOKING FOR PRIVACY AND A PLACE TO RELAX. HE WILL STEP UP TO THE TOILET AND BEGIN WHAT HE HAS BEEN THINKING ABOUT DOING DURING THE LAST TWENTY MINUTES OF CLASS. NOT ONLY WILL PEE SPLASH ALL OVER THE ROOM, IT WILL MOST LIKELY SPRAY THE VICTIM AS WELL.

ADDED BONUS: You could also unscrew the toilet seat, so the victim has to balance on the toilet. Talk about nerve-wracking, especially when drunk!

PRANK UNIVERSITY

011 SOAPY MOUTH

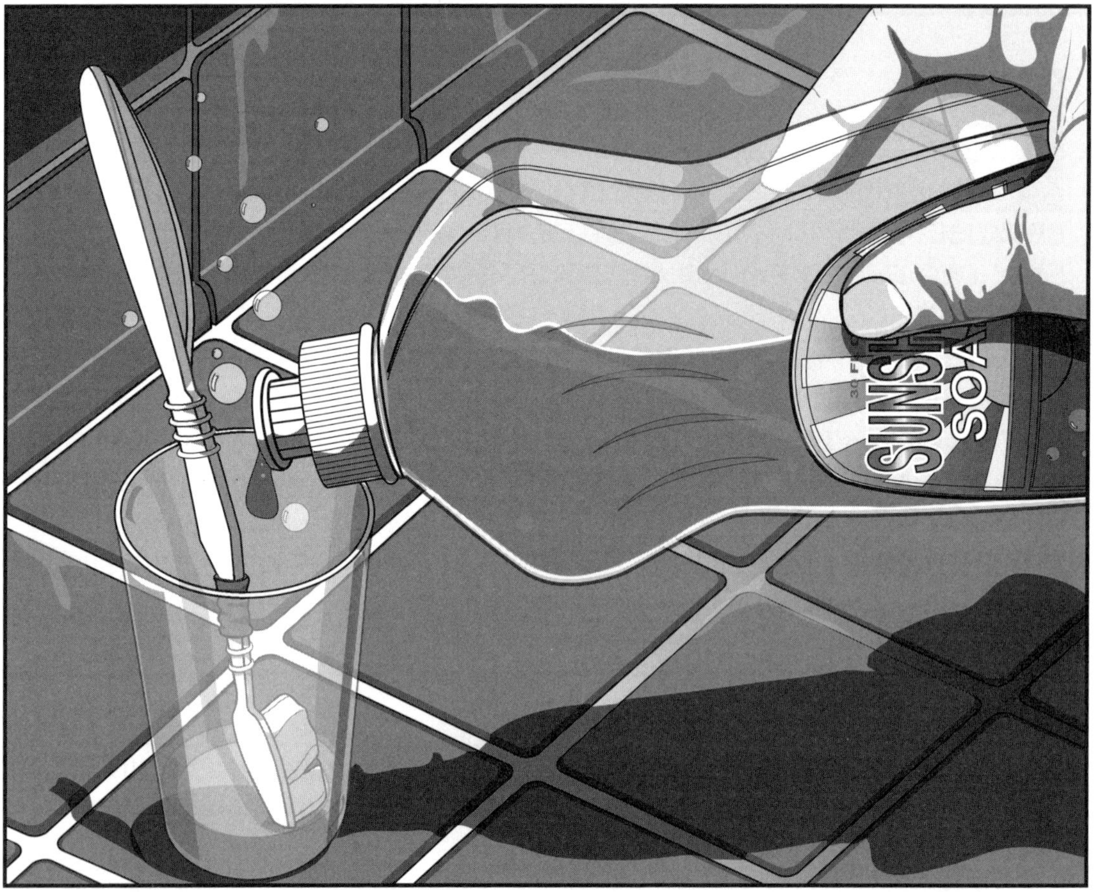

036

SUCCESSFUL ATTEMPTS

1	2	3	4	5	6	7	8	9	10	11	12	13	14	15	16	17

MOST STUDENTS IN COLLEGE TAKE PART IN THE DAILY TASK OF BRUSHING THEIR TEETH—WE HOPE. WELL, REMEMBER WHEN YOUR PARENTS WOULD WASH YOUR MOUTH OUT WITH SOAP? SO, MAYBE YOU NEVER LET THE "F-BOMB" DROP IN FRONT OF YOUR MOM, BUT IT'S AN UNCOMFORTABLE CHILDHOOD EXPERIENCE MANY OF US HAVE GONE THROUGH. NOW YOU CAN HELP YOUR ROOMMATE RELIVE IT. WHEN YOUR ROOMMATE DEPARTS FOR CLASS IN THE MORNING, FILL A CUP FULL OF DISH SOAP. THEN SOAK HIS TOOTHBRUSH IN THE CUP UNTIL DUSK. REMOVE THE BRUSH AND LIGHTLY RINSE ANY OBVIOUS SOAP BUILDUP FROM THE BRISTLES, THEN RETURN THE BRUSH TO ITS ORIGINAL LOCATION AND WAIT. TALK ABOUT A TASTE THAT STAYS IN YOUR MOUTH!

ADDED BONUS: Remember, soap isn't the worst thing the brush could be soaked in!

PRANK UNIVERSITY

012 DRUNK ASS PHOTO

SUCCESSFUL ATTEMPTS

1	2	3	4	5	6	7	8	9	10	11	12	13	14	15	16	17

TAKE A LOOK AT THIS POOR BASTARD: HE ALMOST MADE IT HOME, BUT THEN DECIDED TO TAKE A NAP OUTSIDE IN THE HALL. LITTLE DOES HE KNOW THAT SOMEONE'S BUTT IS WITHIN AN INCH OF HIS FACE AND HIS BUDDIES ARE TAKING PHOTOS. I'M STILL NOT SURE WHO'S REALLY BEING PRANKED IN THIS SCENARIO—IS IT THE GUY SLEEPING QUIETLY, OR IS IT THE GUY WHOSE MAN BUTT WILL BE PLASTERED ALL OVER THE DORM AND THE INTERNET?

ADDED BONUS: Who's heard of the Trojan helmet?

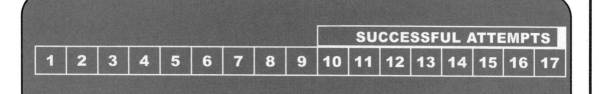

PRANK UNIVERSITY

013 SUPER-SOAKER SINK

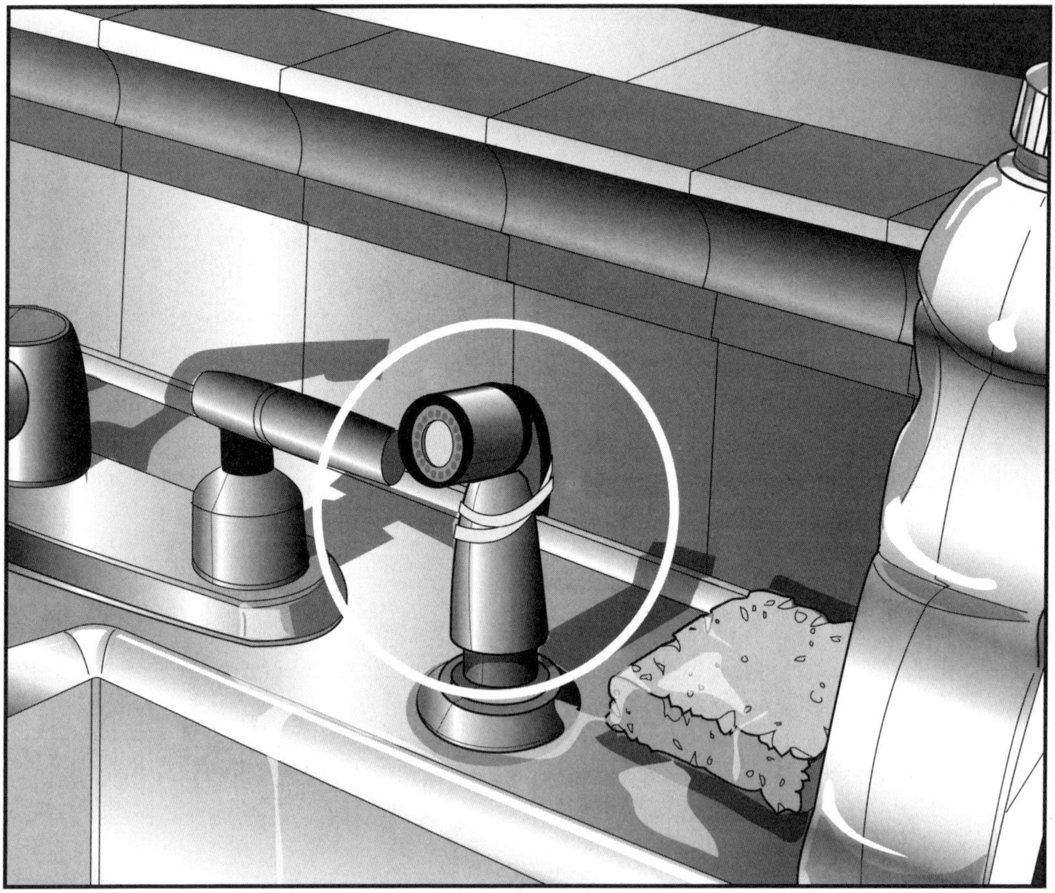

SUCCESSFUL ATTEMPTS

1	2	3	4	5	6	7	8	9	10	11	12	13	14	15	16	17

IMAGINE YOU ARE TAKING A STUDY BREAK AND HAVE WORKED UP A THIRST. YOU DECIDE THAT A BEER IS OUT OF THE QUESTION UNTIL YOU'RE FINISHED STUDYING, SO YOU WALK OVER TO THE SINK FOR A COOL GLASS OF WATER. YOU REACH DOWN AND TURN ON THE FAUCET, AND SUDDENLY A SERIOUS STREAM OF WATER COMES YOUR WAY. YOUR ROOMMATE HAS COME UP WITH SOME KIND OF INGENIOUS INVENTION TO MANIPULATE THE SPRAY NOZZLE TO SPRAY ON COMMAND! HOW DID THAT DUMBASS THINK OF SOMETHING SO SOPHISTICATED? WELL, IT'S REALLY NOT ALL THAT ELABORATE; HE SIMPLY USED A RUBBER BAND.

ADDED BONUS: Black electrical tape also blends nicely with the spray nozzle.

PRANK UNIVERSITY

014 INDUSTRIAL AUTO WRAP

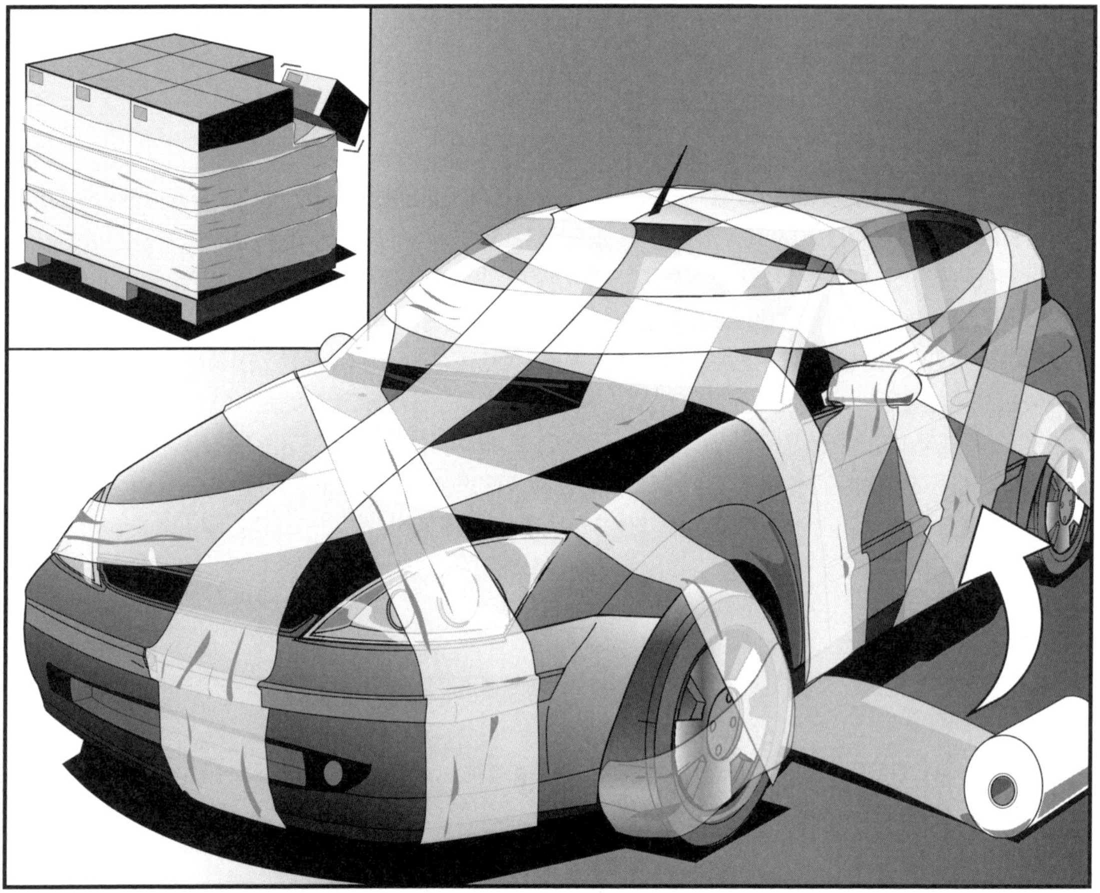

SUCCESSFUL ATTEMPTS

1	2	3	4	5	6	7	8	9	10	11	12	13	14	15	16	17

THERE'S NOTHING LIKE LEAVING FOR WORK AND FINDING YOUR CAR COVERED IN INDUSTRIAL-STRENGTH PLASTIC WRAP—THE SAME PLASTIC WRAP THEY USE TO CONTAIN 100-POUND BOXES WHILE IN TRANSIT. THIS STUFF IS DAMN DURABLE, AND HEAVY. THIS WILL HAVE TO BE A TWO-PERSON JOB, SO FIND A FRIEND, OR MAKE ONE REAL QUICK. MOST LIKELY YOU WILL HAVE TO ORDER THE WRAP FROM A DISTRIBUTOR OF INDUSTRIAL PACKING SUPPLIES. YOU CAN ALSO ASK AROUND AT LOCAL BUSINESSES, AS THEY WILL SOMETIMES GIVE IT TO YOU. THIS PRANK WORKS BEST IF YOU ROLL IN UNDER THE CAR, THEN HAND THE WRAP OVER THE ROOF OF THE AUTO TO YOUR FRIEND. PUT AS MUCH WRAP ON AS YOU WANT, DEPENDING ON HOW MUCH YOU LIKE THE PERSON.

ADDED BONUS: Shaving cream or honey on the car is always a nice surprise.

PRANK UNIVERSITY

015 JELLY SHOES

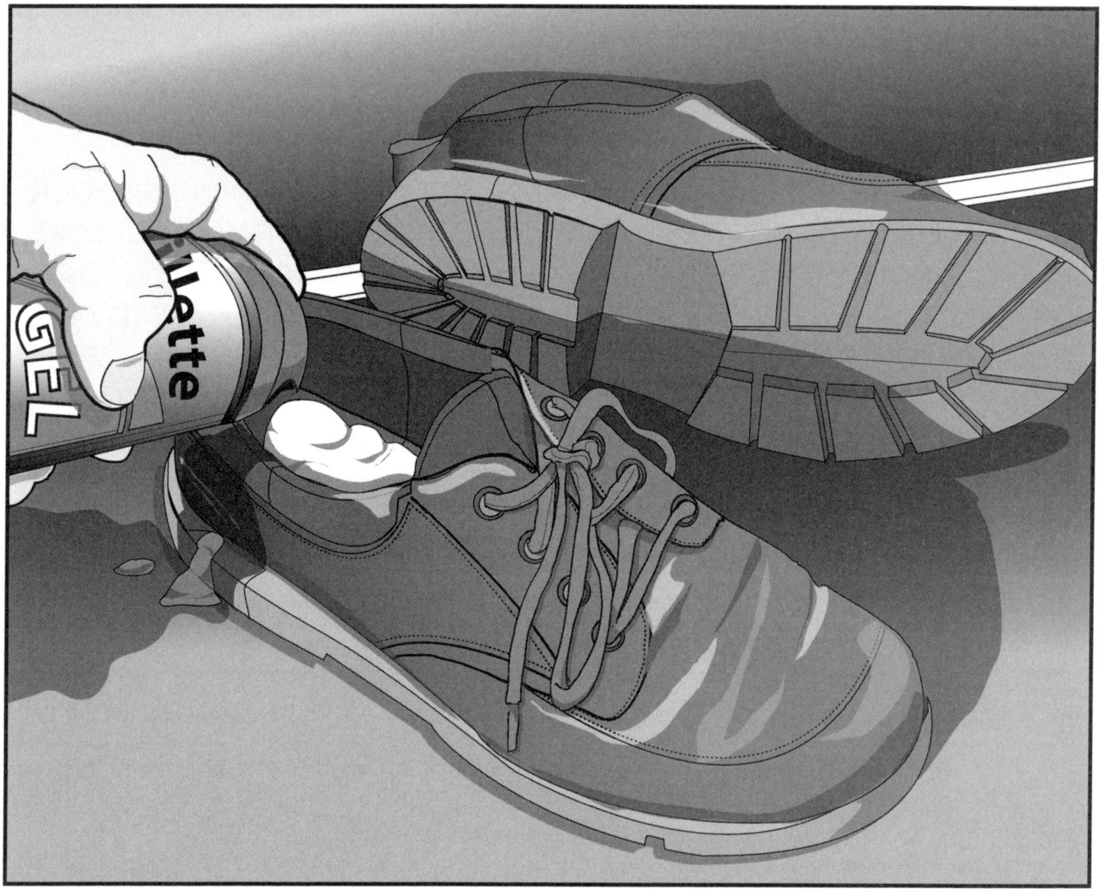

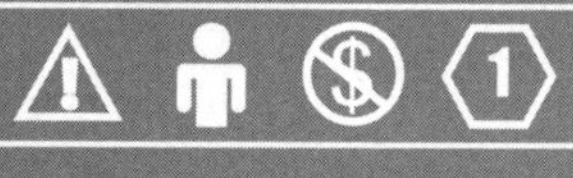

								SUCCESSFUL ATTEMPTS								
1	2	3	4	5	6	7	8	9	10	11	12	13	14	15	16	17

FILLING YOUR ROOMMATE'S SHOES WITH FOREIGN LIQUIDS NEVER GETS OLD. SHAVING CREAM, JELLY, AND LOTION ARE ALL EXCELLENT CHOICES! MAKE SURE YOU HIDE ALL THE LIQUID IN THE TOE AREA. IF YOU HAVE MORE THAN ONE ROOMMATE, YOU CAN EVEN PUT A LITTLE IN YOUR OWN SHOES SO IT APPEARS THAT THE THIRD ROOMMATE IS RESPONSIBLE. (REMEMBER, FRAMING A ROOMMATE IS ALWAYS BETTER THAN TAKING THE BLAME YOURSELF.) THIS PRANK ALSO FITS THE BILL IF YOU FIND YOURSELF IN THE LOCKER ROOM AND FOR SOME REASON YOU HAVE A VENDETTA AGAINST THE FOOTBALL TEAM. A WORD TO THE WISE, THOUGH: DON'T GET CAUGHT BY THEM!

ADDED BONUS: Petroleum jelly works great, but it's a bear to clean out.

PRANK UNIVERSITY

016 PRE-BLEACH

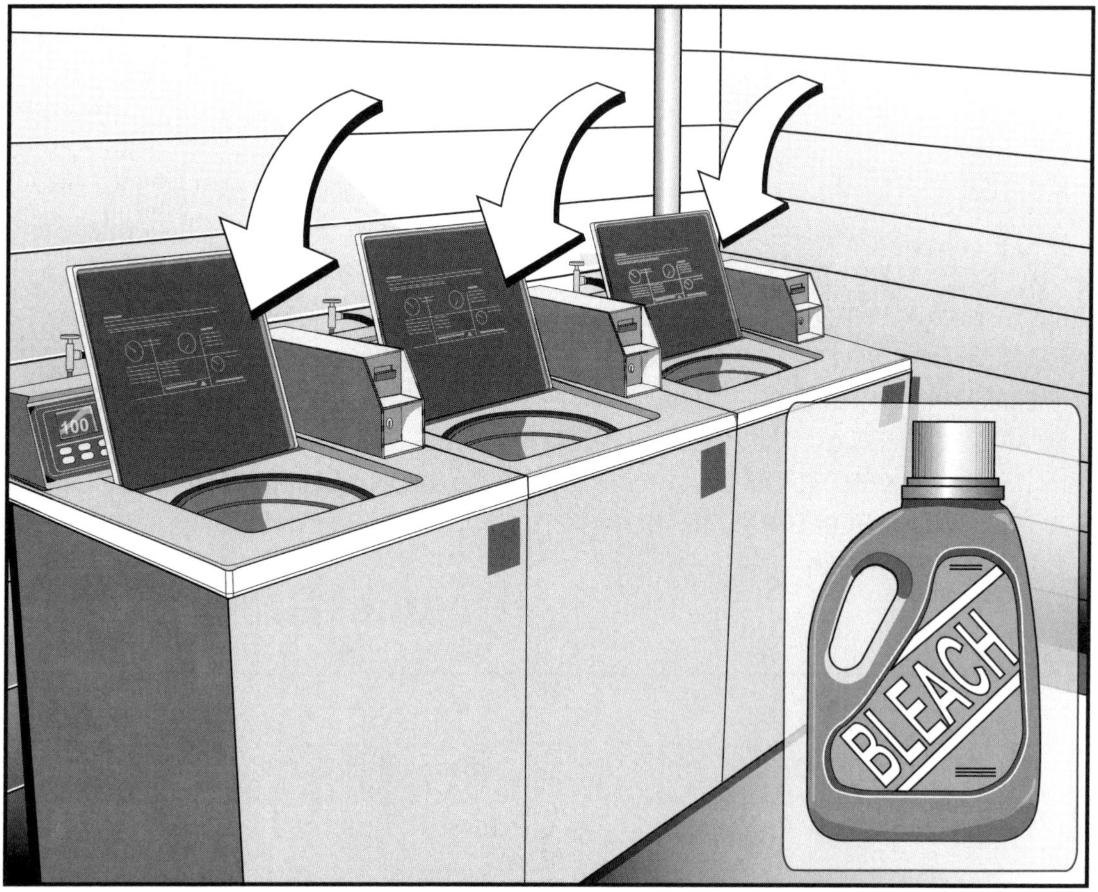

SUCCESSFUL ATTEMPTS

1	2	3	4	5	6	7	8	9	10	11	12	13	14	15	16	17

THE "PRE-BLEACH" CAN TURN A QUIET DORM HALL INTO A RAGING PSYCHOTIC LYNCH MOB! THIS PRANK IS VERY TIME-SENSITIVE, SO MAKE SURE YOU PICK A TIME TO GO DOWN TO THE LAUNDRY ROOM WHEN NO ONE IS THERE. YOU'LL WANT TO PUT AT LEAST A CUP OF BLEACH IN THE MACHINE; THIS ONE WORKS BECAUSE MOST PEOPLE GLANCE IN THE MACHINE, BUT NEVER ASSUME COLOR-ALTERING LIQUIDS ARE LINGERING ON THE BOTTOM.

THIS PRANK IS BENEFICIAL IN TWO WAYS: FIRST, IT PISSES OFF A LOT OF PEOPLE AT ONCE, AND SECOND, YOU'LL KNOW TO STAY CLOSE TO THE WASHING MACHINE WHILE YOUR CLOTHES ARE IN IT. BESIDES, THE LAUNDRY ROOM IS A GREAT PLACE TO GET FRESH WITH THE LADY FOLK!

ADDED BONUS: Chew a whole pack of gum on your way down to the laundry room. Toss the gum into a machine, then quietly walk away.

PRANK UNIVERSITY

017 QUICK LEG SHAVE

SUCCESSFUL ATTEMPTS

1	2	3	4	5	6	7	8	9	10	11	12	13	14	15	16	17

AS YOUR HAIRY-LEGGED ROOMMATE IS SLEEPING, LAY A GOOD-SIZED PIECE OF DUCT TAPE ON HIS LEGS. WHEN HE WAKES UP, HE WILL HAVE TO INFLICT MAJOR PAIN ON HIMSELF AS HE PULLS IT OFF. THERE IS NOTHING SWEETER FOR A PRANKSTER THAN CAUSING A VICTIM SELF-INFLICTED TORTURE! THIS APPLICATION CAN ALSO BE USED FOR YOUR NATURALIST FEMALE ROOMMATE WHO REFUSES TO SHAVE HER LEGS DURING THE WARM MONTHS—THAT'S JUST WRONG. WE RANK THIS PRANK RATHER HIGH, ESPECIALLY IF YOU HAVE THE AUDACITY TO PULL THE TAPE OFF YOURSELF! MENTAL NOTE: IT'S PROBABLY A GOOD THING TO KEEP YOUR DOOR LOCKED AT NIGHT IF YOU "PULL THIS ONE OFF."

ADDED BONUS: Skip the tape and just shave your roommate's legs. The more hair, the more noticeable it will be! It just might take him a few days to notice those beautiful, smooth legs of his.

PRANK UNIVERSITY

018 AUTO ISLAND

									SUCCESSFUL ATTEMPTS							
1	2	3	4	5	6	7	8	9	10	11	12	13	14	15	16	17

IF YOU ARE RENTING A HOUSE WITH A GROUP OF GUYS, MOST LIKELY SOMEONE HAS TO PARK ON THE GRASS. (MOST OFF-CAMPUS HOMES WERE ONCE SINGLE-FAMILY HOMES AND HAVE BEEN CONVERTED INTO COLLEGE HOUSING, AND EVERY STUDENT LIVING THERE HAS A CAR.) LATE ONE NIGHT, WITH THE HELP OF A FRIEND, DIG A ONE-AND-A-HALF-FOOT HOLE IN FRONT OF AND BEHIND THE CAR'S TIRES. YOU DON'T HAVE TO DIG A HOLE AROUND THE ENTIRE VEHICLE; A CAR CAN ONLY GO FORWARD OR BACKWARD. MOST COUPES AND SEDANS WON'T BE ABLE TO HANDLE THE HOLE, SO THE DRIVER WILL HAVE TO WALK OR BORROW SOMEONE ELSE'S CAR.

ADDED BONUS: Fill the hole with water, so it appears to be a puddle.

PRANK UNIVERSITY

019 LAWN-ORNAMENT SWITCH

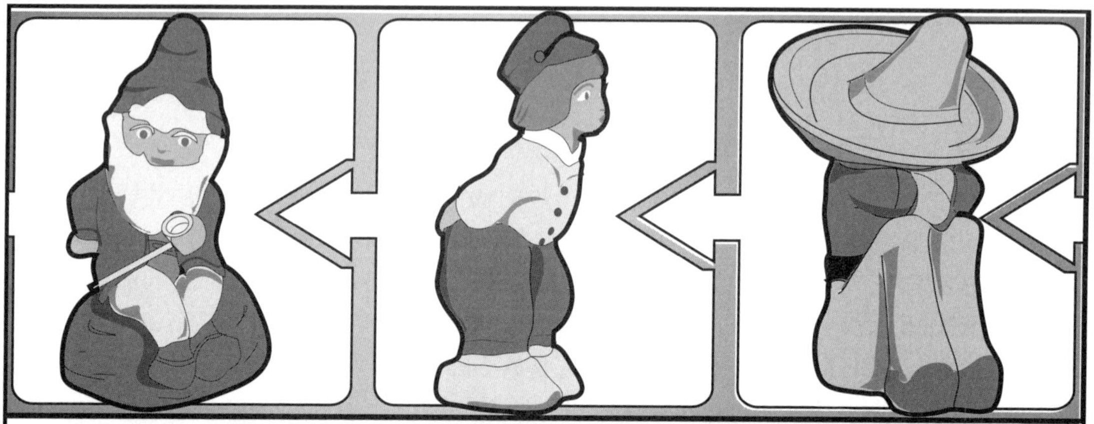

SUCCESSFUL ATTEMPTS

1	2	3	4	5	6	7	8	9	10	11	12	13	14	15	16	17

THERE ISN'T MUCH TO DO AT 2:30 IN THE MORNING. IF YOU AND YOUR FRIENDS HAVE SOME AMBITION, TRY THIS ONE OUT: TAKE A LAWN ORNAMENT FROM ONE HOUSE AND DROP IT OFF AT THE NEXT HOUSE. KEEP DOING THIS DOWN AN ENTIRE STREET. FOR THE NEXT WEEK, NEIGHBORS WILL BE CURIOUS AS TO WHY THEIR CONCRETE FROG HAS TURNED INTO A GARDEN GNOME. THIS PRANK REALLY GIVES NEIGHBORS A CHANCE TO MINGLE, SO YOU'RE DOING COMMUNITY SERVICE!

ADDED BONUS: The holidays are an excellent time to pull this prank. Remove Christmas decorations from one house, and adorn the grinch's next door!

PRANK UNIVERSITY

020 NUMBER 2 FOREVER

054

SUCCESSFUL ATTEMPTS

1	2	3	4	5	6	7	8	9	10	11	12	13	14	15	16	17

THIS IS A GREAT WAY TO USE YOUR OLD SHOES AND BOOTS! IF YOU HAVE A PAIR OF OLD SHOES, ROLL UP SOME NEWSPAPER, PLACE TUBE SOCKS OVER THE ROLLS, AND STICK THEM INTO THE SHOES. THEN, PLACE THEM IN THE HALL BATHROOM. MAKE SURE YOU LOCK THE STALL DOOR. YOU WOULDN'T WANT ANYONE WALKING IN ON YOUR SIZE TWELVES WHEN "YOU" ARE DROPPING A DEUCE. IT'S IMPORTANT THAT YOU KEEP THIS PRANK ON THE DOWN-LOW; THAT WAY MORE PEOPLE WILL FALL FOR IT. REMEMBER THAT SHOES ARE EXTRA CHEAP AT SECONDHAND STORES IF YOU DON'T WANT TO BE FINGERED AS THE CULPRIT.

ADDED BONUS: If you add some pants to the shoes, it will look so believable that they will probably sit there for a week. Good luck!

PRANK UNIVERSITY

021 NEW GREETING

SUCCESSFUL ATTEMPTS

1	2	3	4	5	6	7	8	9	10	11	12	13	14	15	16	17

AS SIMPLE AS THIS PRANK MAY SOUND, YOU CAN REALLY HAVE A LOT OF FUN WITH IT. HOW OFTEN DO YOU CALL YOUR OWN PHONE OR HEAR YOUR OWN GREETING? WHEN YOU'RE VISITING A FRIEND'S ROOM AND HE OR SHE STEPS OUT FOR A SECOND, MAKE YOUR MOVE. QUICKLY RECORD A NEW MESSAGE THAT IS BOTH VULGAR AND PROFANE. BUT DON'T MAKE IT TOO AWFUL, BECAUSE THAT DUDE'S MOM IS GOING TO CALL ONE OF THESE DAYS. ALSO, IF IT'S TOO WEIRD, PEOPLE WILL COMMENT ABOUT IT ON THE MACHINE, WHICH WILL RESULT IN SUSPICION, AND ULTIMATELY HE OR SHE WILL LISTEN TO IT AND CHANGE IT!

ADDED BONUS: Record a guy's voice on someone else's girlfriend's machine: "Busy with Susan, please call back." Awesomely done.

PRANK UNIVERSITY

022 DOORBELL DRENCH

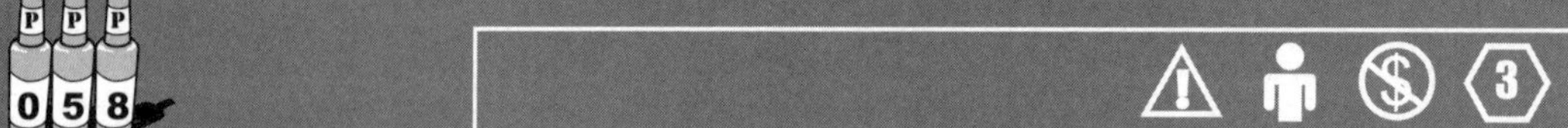

SUCCESSFUL ATTEMPTS

1	2	3	4	5	6	7	8	9	10	11	12	13	14	15	16	17

THIS PRANK IS REQUIRED FOR ALL COLLEGE STUDENTS. IT WILL ONLY WORK ON A DOOR THAT OPENS INWARD, THOUGH. FIND A NEIGHBOR YOU OCCASIONALLY DISLIKE. ROUND UP A GARBAGE CAN OR THE DORM RECYCLING BIN AND FILL IT WITH WATER. LEAN IT AGAINST THE DOOR AT AN ANGLE (SEE IMAGE). NOW, KNOCK ON THE DOOR AND RUN LIKE HELL! REMEMBER NOT TO SLAM YOUR OWN DOOR IF YOU GO INTO YOUR ROOM, BECAUSE IF THEY HEAR YOU THEY'LL BE ABLE TO FIGURE OUT WHO THE PRANKSTER IS PRETTY EASILY. AS THE ANNOYING NEIGHBOR OPENS THE DOOR, THE PAIL WILL FALL INWARD AND UNLOAD ITS CONTENTS ALL OVER THE CARPET! THE FLOOR WILL ABSORB THE LIQUID AND THE UNPLEASANT MOISTURE WILL STICK AROUND FOR SEVERAL DAYS.

ADDED BONUS: You can also mix solids with that water. For example, popcorn kernels are a total pain to clean up and are really cheap to buy.

PRANK UNIVERSITY

023 T.P.

SUCCESSFUL ATTEMPTS

1	2	3	4	5	6	7	8	9	10	11	12	13	14	15	16	17

ON THE INTERNET, CHEAP TOILET PAPER RUNS AROUND FORTY DOLLARS FOR A CASE OF NINETY-SIX ROLLS. WITH THAT SMALL INVESTMENT, YOU CAN REALLY DECK OUT A HOUSE! IF YOU WENT TO HIGH SCHOOL, YOU KNOW WHAT THIS IS ALL ABOUT. ROUND UP A CASE OF TOILET PAPER, CONVINCE SOMEONE TO BE YOUR DRIVER, AND YOU'RE OFF! SNEAK UP TO A HOUSE AND START THROWING. IF YOU GET CAUGHT YOU MAY HAVE TO CLEAN UP ANY MESS YOU MAKE, SO TRY NOT TO BREAK ANYTHING. ALSO, YOU REALLY SHOULD HAVE SOMEONE FILMING THIS. IT'S TOO GOOD NOT TO RECORD. ASSAULT YOUR FRIENDS' HOUSES WHEN THEY ARE OUT AT THE BAR—THERE'S NOTHING LIKE COMING HOME DRUNK TO A WHITE CHRISTMAS.

ADDED BONUS: Soak the paper in puddles for the world's biggest spitballs!

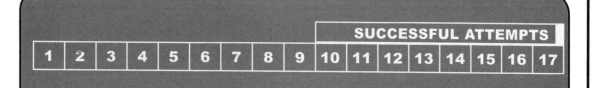

PRANK UNIVERSITY

024 DIXIE SURPRISE

062

SUCCESSFUL ATTEMPTS

1	2	3	4	5	6	7	8	9	10	11	12	13	14	15	16	17

YOUR DORM NEIGHBOR HAS GONE OUT FOR THE NIGHT AND WILL PROBABLY NOT BE RETURNING BEFORE THE BAR CLOSES. AS SOON AS HE EMBARKS ON HIS MISSION, RUN TO THE LOCAL SUPERMARKET AND LOAD UP ON SMALL DIXIE CUPS. YOU'LL NEED A FEW HUNDRED OF THEM FOR THIS PRANK. STARTING FROM THE BACK OF THE ROOM, PLACE CUPS FILLED WITH WATER WITHIN INCHES OF ONE ANOTHER TILL YOU REACH THE DOOR. FOR EVEN MORE INSULT, UNSCREW THE LIGHTBULB. COME 3 A.M., THE NEIGHBOR COMES HOME, TOTALLY WASTED. IT'S PITCH BLACK AND THERE'S MISCHIEF IN THE AIR. BOOZE BOY STARTS TO ENTER HIS ROOM, ONLY TO FIND HIMSELF IN A HORRIBLE DIXIE-CUP NIGHTMARE AS HE BEGINS TO TRIP OVER THEM.

ADDED BONUS: Staple the cups together as you place them next to one another. This creation is almost impossible to clean up without making a mess.

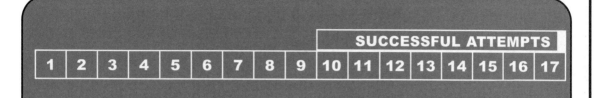

PRANK UNIVERSITY

025 SIDEWALK CHANGE

SUCCESSFUL ATTEMPTS

1	2	3	4	5	6	7	8	9	10	11	12	13	14	15	16	17

THIS PRANK IS ONE OF THE BEST TO FILM. YOU WILL NEED A GOOD LOCATION, SUCH AS A HEAVILY TRAFFICKED SIDEWALK. ALSO, MAKE SURE YOUR CAMERAMAN DOESN'T HAVE ANYTHING OBSTRUCTING HIS LINE OF SIGHT. YOU SHOULD PROBABLY SET UP TWO LOCATIONS; THAT WAY, IF ONE OF THE LOCATIONS IS DEAD, YOUR CAMERAMAN CAN QUICKLY ZOOM IN ON THE OTHER. REMEMBER: OLD PEOPLE STOP FOR ANYTHING, BUT YOUNG PEOPLE WILL ONLY STOP FOR DIMES AND QUARTERS. YOU SHOULD USE A STRONG GLUE TO HOLD THE CHANGE DOWN. SOMETHING ABOUT TWO OLD LADIES KICKING AT A QUARTER FOR TEN MINUTES NEVER GETS OLD!

ADDED BONUS: An indoor location—a school hallway, or on the steps—can be just as good, but these locations are hard to capture on film.

PRANK UNIVERSITY

026 AIR-HORN ALARM

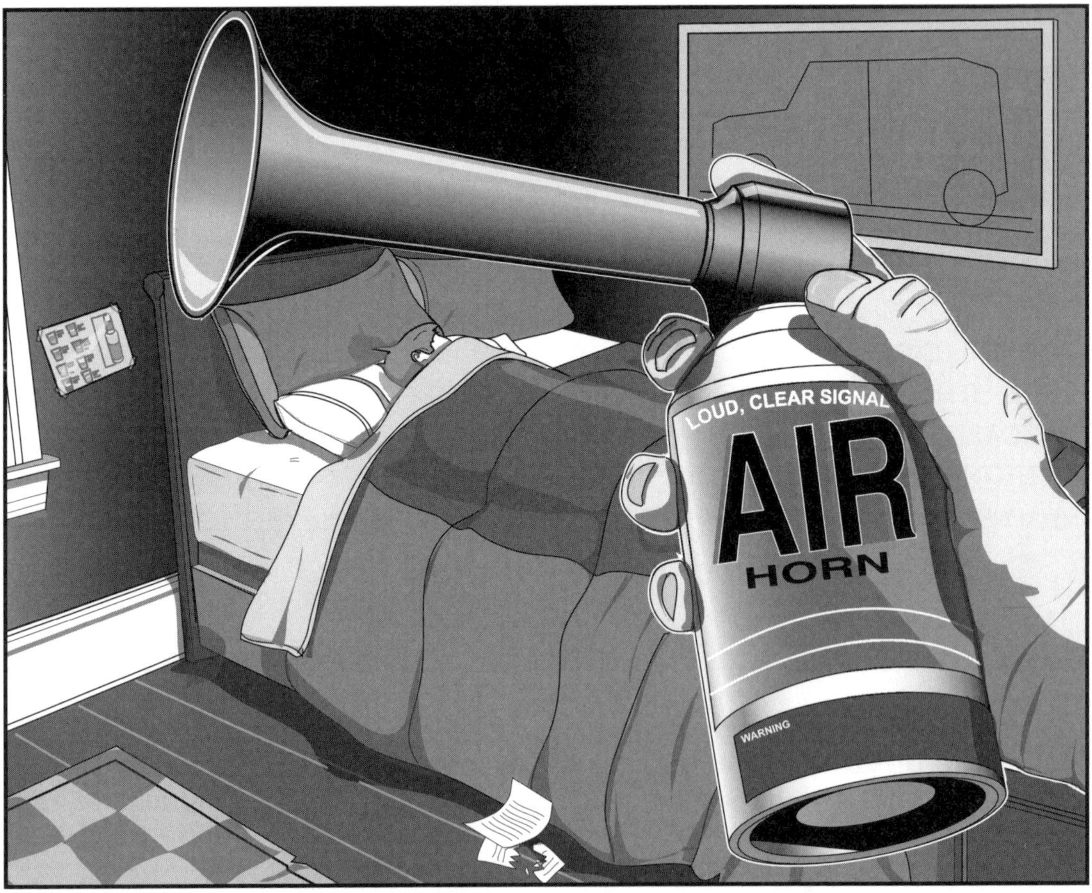

SUCCESSFUL ATTEMPTS

1	2	3	4	5	6	7	8	9	10	11	12	13	14	15	16	17

YOUR ROOMMATE DID IT AGAIN—HE STAYED UP TOO LATE LAST NIGHT AND HAS DECIDED TO SLEEP IN THIS MORNING. HE SHOULD NEVER HAVE SIGNED UP FOR CLASSES AT 8 A.M., BUT HE DID, AND WILL PROBABLY HAVE TO RETAKE THEM NEXT SEMESTER. YOU ARE VERY CONCERNED WITH HIS ACADEMIC PERFORMANCE AND DECIDE TO TAKE THINGS INTO YOUR OWN HANDS. HE IS QUIETLY SLEEPING WHEN OUT OF NOWHERE COME 120 DECIBELS OF AIR HORN. MAKE SURE YOU STAND AT LEAST TEN FEET FROM HIM, OR YOU'LL BLOW HIS EARDRUMS!

ADDED BONUS: Run down the hallway with the air horn and yell, "Wake up! Earthquake drill!"

PRANK UNIVERSITY

027 ITCHY SHEETS

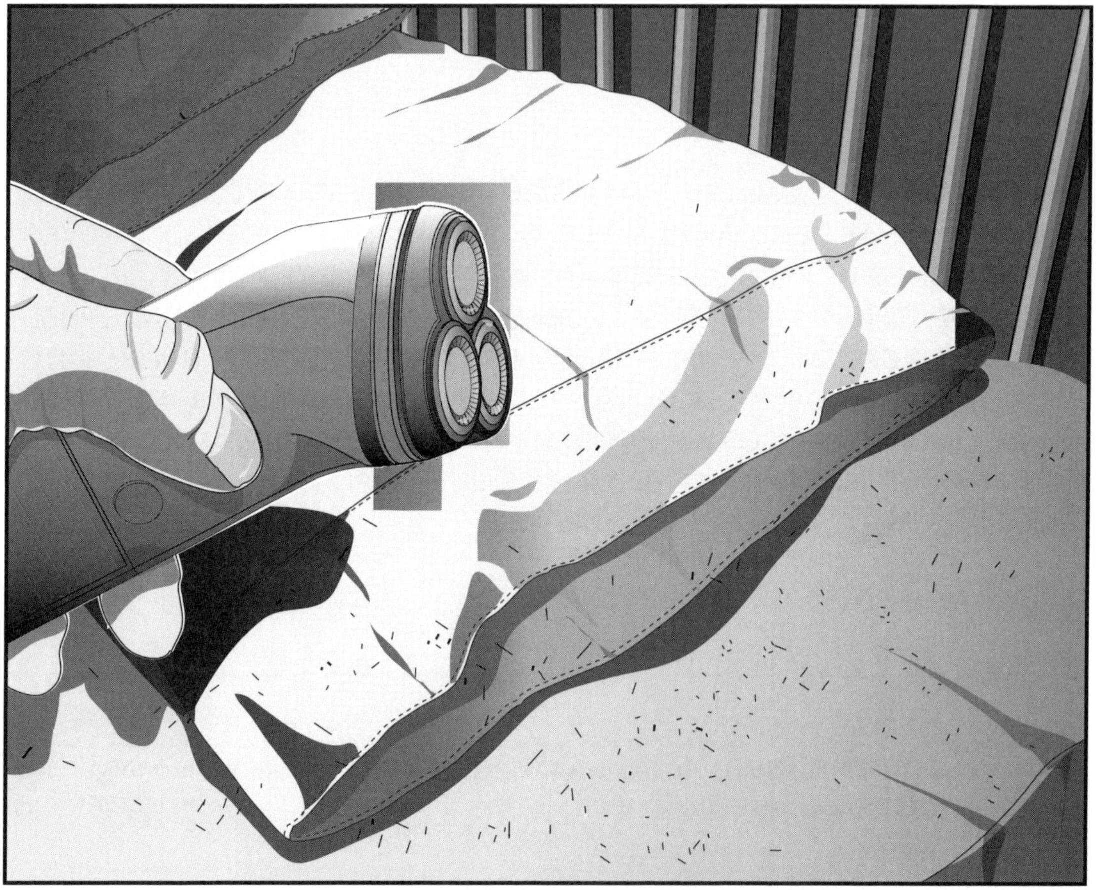

SUCCESSFUL ATTEMPTS

1	2	3	4	5	6	7	8	9	10	11	12	13	14	15	16	17

YOUR ROOMMATE HAS JUST RETURNED FROM PLAYING A GAME OF QUARTERS. HE LOOKS LIKE HE'S HAD ONE TOO MANY AGAIN AND IS DESPERATE TO PASS OUT. HE MAKES IT TO HIS BED AND QUICKLY UNDRESSES. AS HE SETTLES IN, HE BEGINS TO ITCH. FOR SOME REASON, THERE ARE THOUSANDS OF LITTLE WHISKERS IN HIS BED. HE WILL PROBABLY TOSS AND TURN ALL NIGHT! HIS ONLY OTHER OPTION IS TO REMOVE THE SHEETS AND JUST SLEEP ON THE MATTRESS, WHICH WE ALL KNOW IS VERY UNCOMFORTABLE AND SUCKS LIKE HELL, AND HE'S PROBABLY TOO DRUNK TO PULL THAT OFF ANYWAY.

ADDED BONUS: Adding your whiskers to the inside of a T-shirt also works.

PRANK UNIVERSITY

028 DIRTY TOWEL

SUCCESSFUL ATTEMPTS

1	2	3	4	5	6	7	8	9	10	11	12	13	14	15	16	17

FIRST, YOU WILL WANT TO HIDE ALL THE TOWELS IN THE BATHROOM, EXCEPT FOR ONE. TAKE A CONTAINER OF PETROLEUM JELLY AND SMEAR IT ALL OVER THE BACKSIDE OF THE ONLY TOWEL LEFT ON THE TOWEL RACK. YOU WILL WANT TO COVER EVERY INCH, BUT MAKE SURE YOUR ROOMMATES CAN'T SEE THE HIGH-GLOSS REFLECTION IT GIVES OFF. YOUR POOR VICTIM WILL START TO DRY HIS HANDS ON THE TOWEL, ONLY TO FIND THEM CAKED IN PETROLEUM JELLY. IT'S A PAIN TO REMOVE FROM YOUR HANDS—YOU PRACTICALLY HAVE TO SCRAPE IT OFF! HE'LL BE SO PISSED, HE WILL PROBABLY DECIDE TO HUNT YOU DOWN AND WIPE IT ON YOU, OR—MORE FRIGHTENINGLY—YOUR BED. YOU MIGHT AS WELL THROW THE TOWEL, AND YOUR SHEETS, AWAY AFTER THIS ONE.

ADDED BONUS: Better yet, break open a ballpoint pen and empty it on the backside of the towel.

PRANK UNIVERSITY

029 DUCHESS ADS

SUCCESSFUL ATTEMPTS

1	2	3	4	5	6	7	8	9	10	11	12	13	14	15	16	17

COLLEGE IS A PLACE FOR PARTYING, STUDYING, AND AVOIDING STUDYING. IT IS A PLACE WHERE FAST FOOD IS EATEN AND THE CONVERSATION IS ABOUT LAST NIGHT'S DATES. IT'S TIME TO BE USEFUL. WHEN YOU AND YOUR ROOMMATE HAVE SOME FREE TIME, START ACCUMULATING AS MANY FREE MAGAZINES AS POSSIBLE. START RIPPING OUT THE PAGES—THE MORE ADS FEATURING FEMININE-HYGIENE PRODUCTS, THE BETTER. I'M TALKING ABOUT HUNDREDS OF THEM! SNEAK INTO YOUR FRIEND'S HOUSE OR ROOM AND START PAPERING THE WALLS. MAKE SURE YOU COVER EVERY SQUARE INCH. YOU WILL PROBABLY ONLY PULL THIS PRANK ONCE, SO MAKE SURE YOU DO IT RIGHT! PUT THEM EVERYWHERE IN THE HOUSE—THE FRIDGE, THE TOILET, AND THE SHOWER.

ADDED BONUS: If you have something against tearing up magazines, yellow sticky notes also work great for this prank—but that's a lot more boring.

PRANK UNIVERSITY

030 SIT DOWN/STAND UP

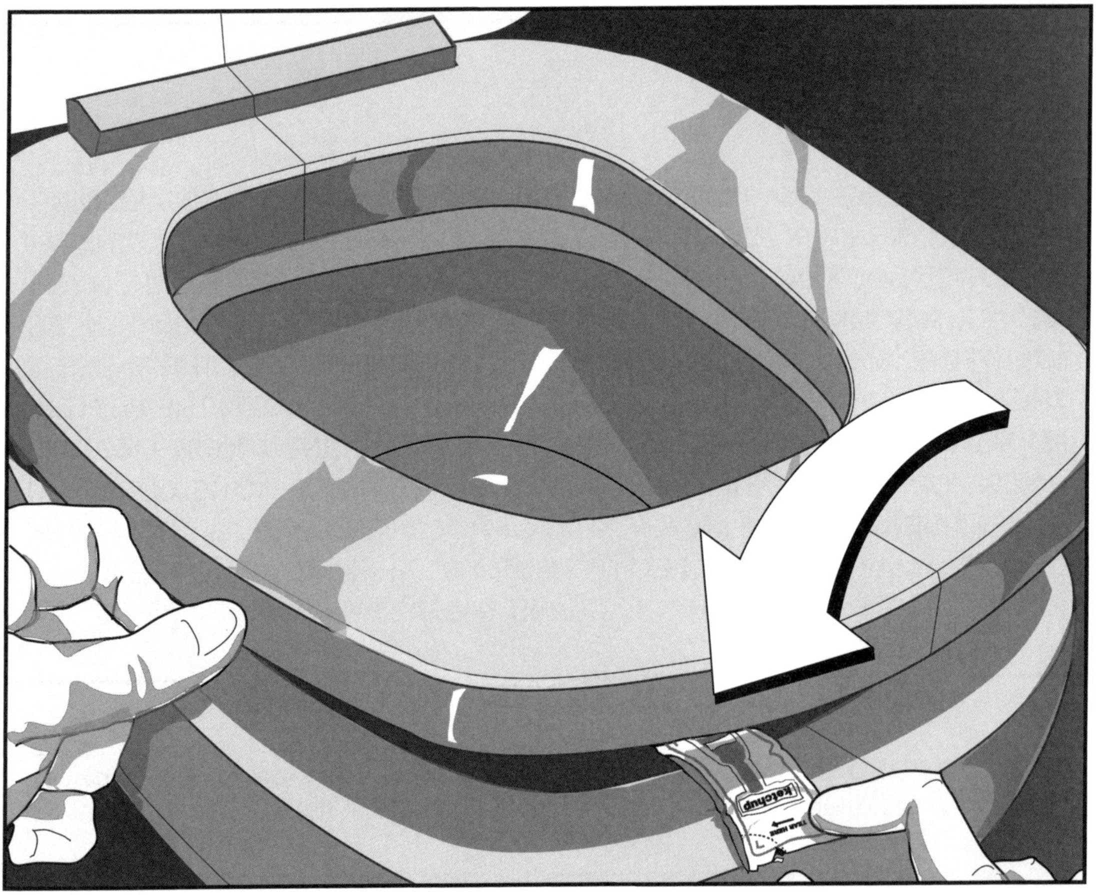

3

SUCCESSFUL ATTEMPTS																
1	2	3	4	5	6	7	8	9	10	11	12	13	14	15	16	17

RESTAURANTS ALWAYS GIVE YOU TOO MANY OF THOSE CONDIMENT PACKETS, AND THEY ARE OFTEN THROWN AWAY, UNUSED. START TO COLLECT THEM, AS I HAVE A GREAT USE FOR THEM: TEAR THE CORNER OFF A PACKET AND PLACE IT UNDER THE TOILET SEAT. WHEN SOME POOR INDIVIDUAL SITS DOWN, HE OR SHE WILL COMPRESS THE PACKET, AND KETCHUP WILL SQUIRT ALL OVER THEIR LEGS. SOMETIMES THE SIMPLE TASK OF GOING TO THE BATHROOM CAN BECOME THE BIGGEST BLUNDER OF THE DAY. THIS PRANK WORKS BEST FOR ON-CAMPUS RESTROOMS AND WORK ENVIRONMENTS!

ADDED BONUS: Skip all that, and just squirt ketchup in the toilet. That will pretty much gross anyone out!

PRANK UNIVERSITY

031 CURTAIN REMOVAL

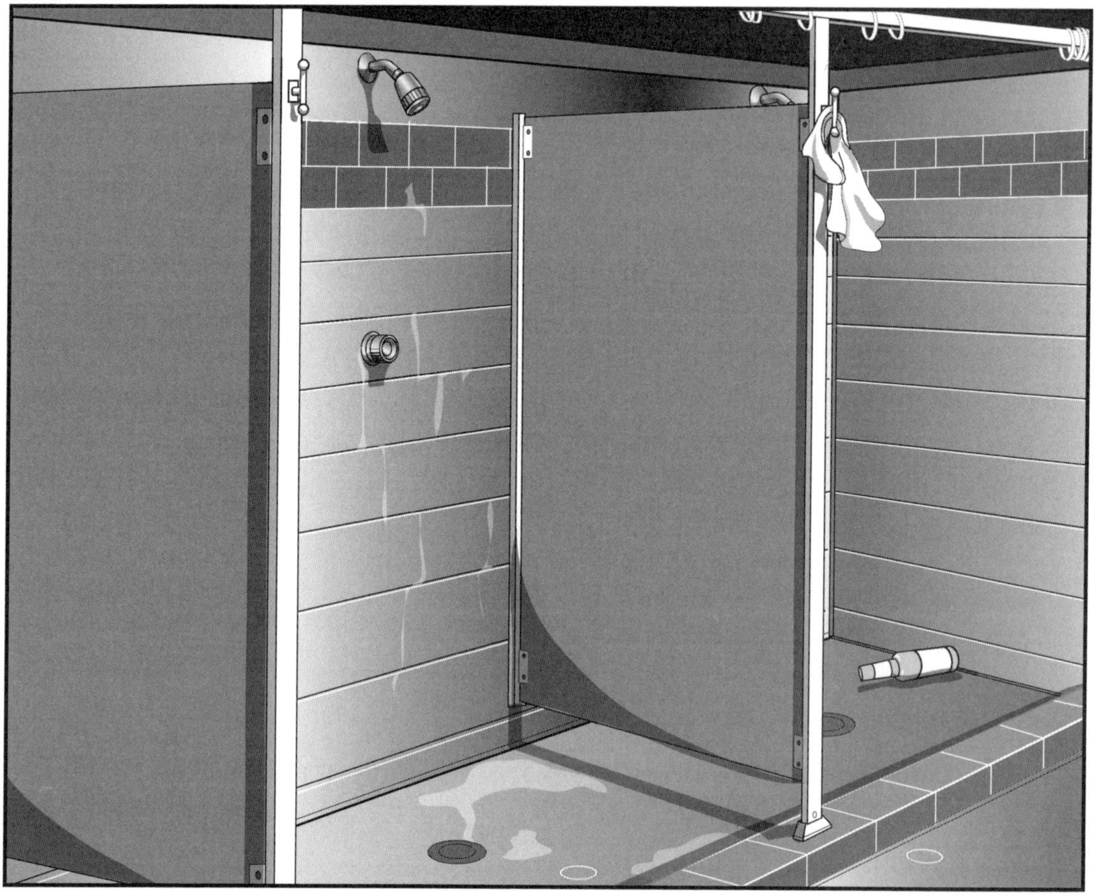

SUCCESSFUL ATTEMPTS

1	2	3	4	5	6	7	8	9	10	11	12	13	14	15	16	17

THIS ONE IS FAIRLY SIMPLE TO UNDERSTAND. IF YOU LIVE IN THE DORMS, RUN UP TO THE NEXT FLOOR AND REMOVE ALL THE SHOWER CURTAINS. YOU MIGHT WANT TO WEAR HAND PROTECTION, AS THOSE CURTAINS COULD BE FILLED WITH ALL KINDS OF FUNGAL INFECTIONS YOU DON'T WANT! ALSO, YOU WILL WANT TO MAKE SURE THAT THE SHOWERS ARE EMPTY—GETTING A REPUTATION AS "MR. PEEPERS" WILL KILL YOUR LOVE LIFE. THE NEXT MORNING, YOUR DORMMATES WILL GET UNDRESSED, GRAB THEIR LITTLE SHOWER CADDIES, AND WALK INTO THE SHOWER, ONLY TO FIND A CURTAINLESS BOX. THIS IS A REAL TEST FOR PROPER PUBLIC SHOWER ETIQUETTE AND WANDERING-EYE TENDENCIES.

ADDED BONUS: Place clues around campus to help the janitorial staff locate where you and your friends hid the precious shower-curtain stash.

PRANK UNIVERSITY

032 PILLOWCASE MOUSE

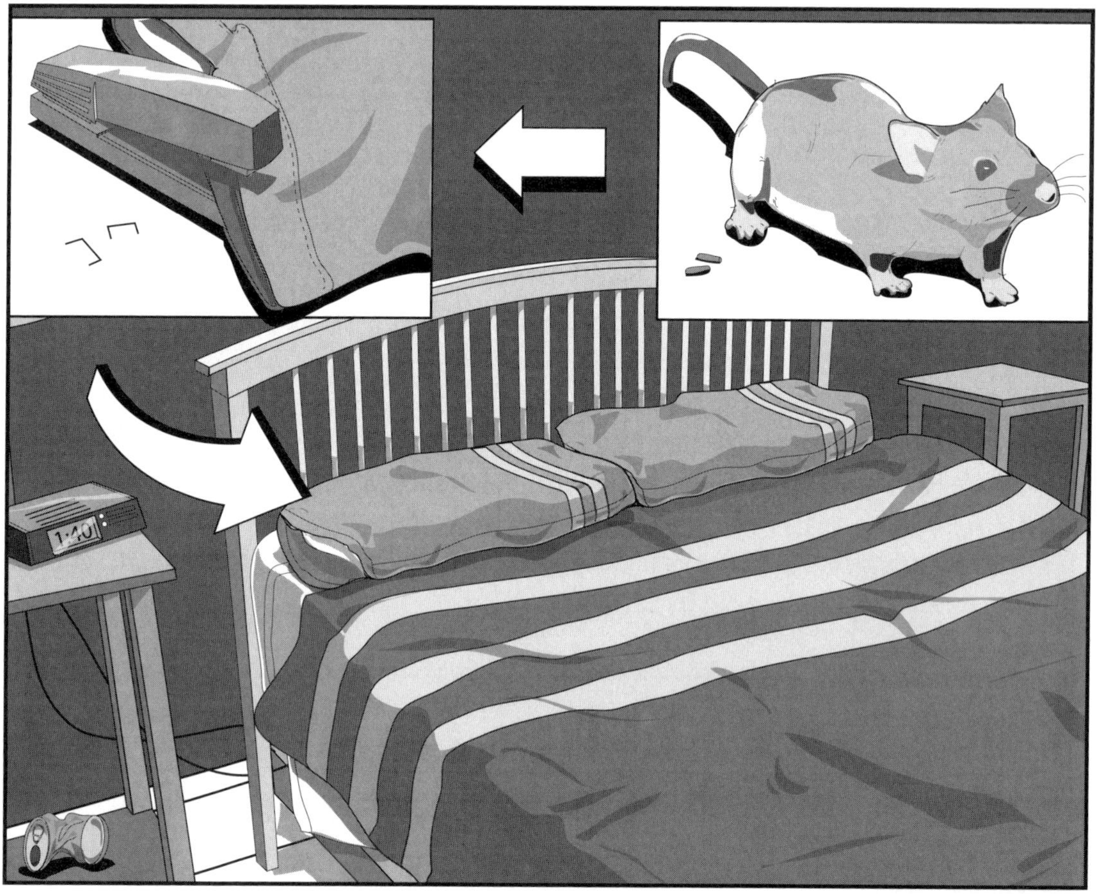

SUCCESSFUL ATTEMPTS

1	2	3	4	5	6	7	8	9	10	11	12	13	14	15	16	17

THIS PRANK IS TIME-SENSITIVE. YOU WILL NEED TO PULL IT OFF WITHIN TWO HOURS OF THE PRANKEE'S BEDTIME. GO PURCHASE A SMALL MOUSE AT YOUR LOCAL PET STORE. PUT THE MOUSE INSIDE THE VICTIM'S PILLOWCASE. NOW, FOLD THE OPEN END OVER AND STAPLE IT SHUT. DO NOT STAPLE THE MOUSE! TIME IS OF THE ESSENCE BECAUSE IF THIS TASK IS DONE TOO EARLY, THE MOUSE WILL EAT HIS WAY OUT OF THE PILLOWCASE. THE OWNER OF THE PILLOWCASE WILL LIE DOWN TO SLEEP AND BEGIN TO HEAR SOMETHING RUNNING AROUND IN THE PILLOW. IF IT'S A GIRL, SHE WILL PROBABLY HAVE NIGHTMARES ALL YEAR. NOW REMEMBER, IF YOU DO THIS TO YOUR ROOMMATE AND THE MOUSE GETS AWAY, YOU WILL HAVE A MOUSE IN THE HOUSE!

ADDED BONUS: Squirt a little water under the pillowcase. After the prank, it will look like the mouse piddled during all the commotion.

PRANK UNIVERSITY

033 REDNECK PARKING BRAKE

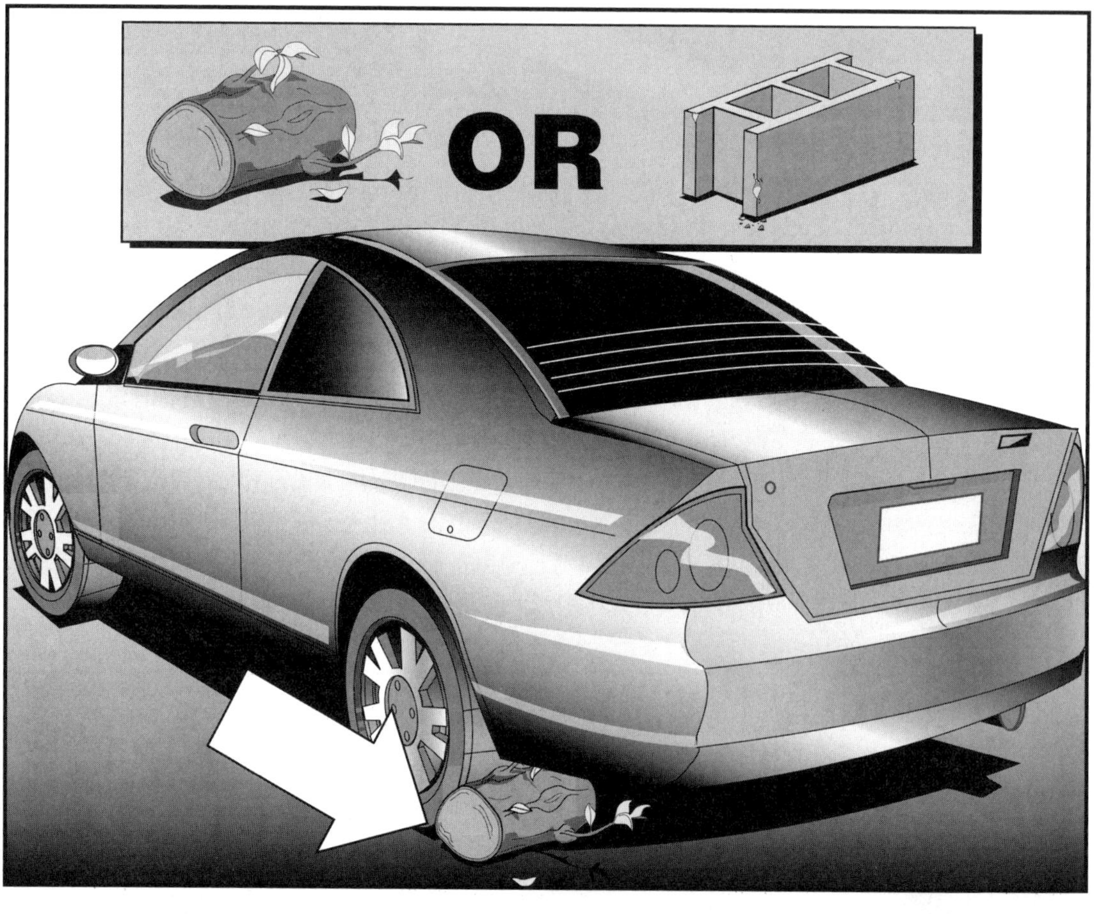

SUCCESSFUL ATTEMPTS

1	2	3	4	5	6	7	8	9	10	11	12	13	14	15	16	17

TO PULL OFF THIS PRANK, YOU WILL NEED TO FIGURE OUT HOW THE DRIVER IS GOING TO APPROACH HIS OR HER VEHICLE. AFTER YOU HAVE DETERMINED THEIR LINE OF SIGHT, PLACE LOGS BEHIND THE TIRES SO THE VICTIM CANNOT SEE THEM. FOR EXAMPLE, IF THE DRIVER IS APPROACHING HER CAR FROM THE DRIVER'S SIDE AND WILL NEED TO BACK OUT, YOU WILL WANT TO PLACE A LOG BEHIND EACH OF THE PASSENGER-SIDE TIRES. SHE WILL PROBABLY DO ONE OF THREE THINGS: SHE WILL ROCK BACK AND FORTH, GET OUT THINKING SOMETHING IS BROKEN ON HER CAR, OR "GIVE IT HELL" TILL SHE BECOMES UNSTUCK. IF YOU HAVE THE AMBITION, FIND A CORD OF WOOD AND A HUGE PARKING LOT. WHEN UNDERGOING A TASK OF THIS MAGNITUDE, IT'S BEST IF YOU BECOME A SHADOW, AND STAY OUT OF SIGHT.

ADDED BONUS: An aluminum can behind each tire is also fun.

PRANK UNIVERSITY

034 SILLY-STRING SLEEP

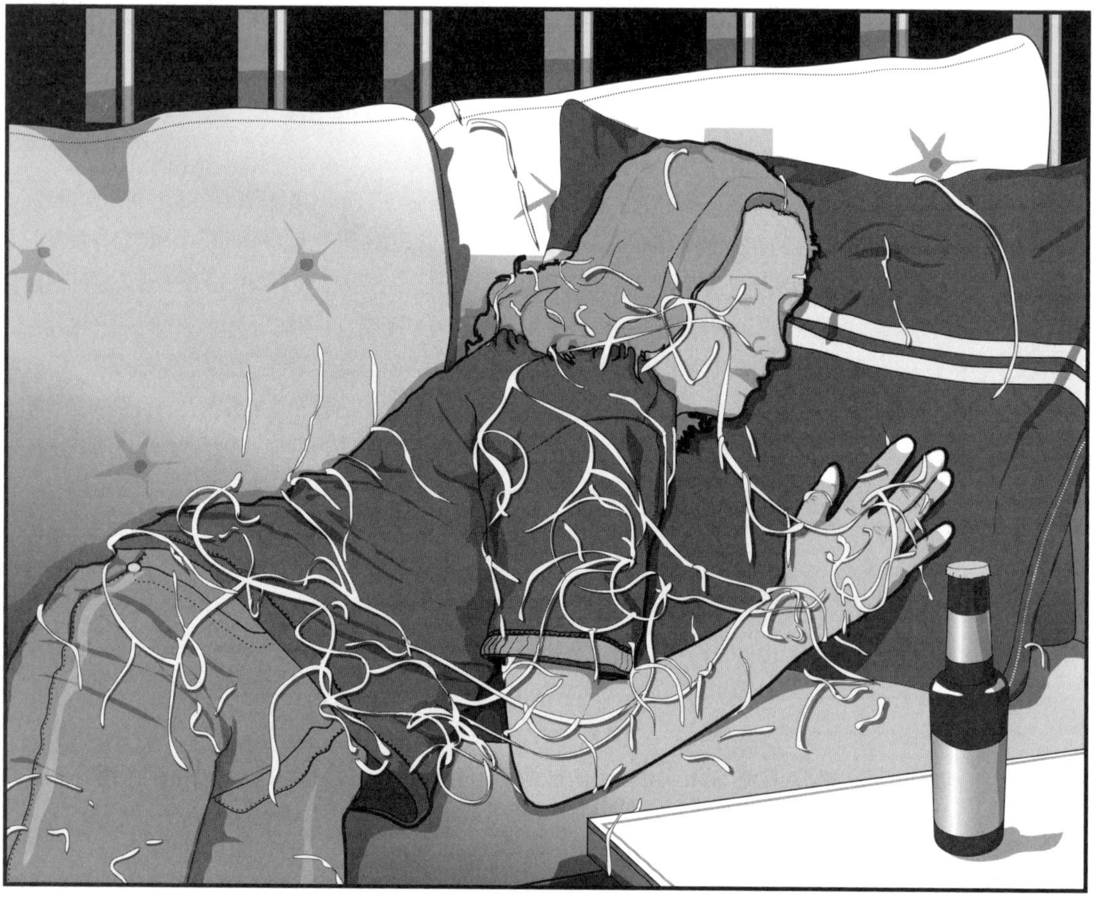

SUCCESSFUL ATTEMPTS

1	2	3	4	5	6	7	8	9	10	11	12	13	14	15	16	17

HEY, DUMBASS, IF YOU'RE TIRED, GO TO BED! DON'T FALL ASLEEP ON THE COUCH IN FRONT OF EVERYONE! IF YOU DECIDE TO PASS OUT IN THE LIVING ROOM, YOU DESERVE TO BE PENALIZED. IN THIS BOOK, WE DISCUSS SEVERAL "PENALTIES" FOR CRASHING IN PUBLIC, BUT ONE QUICK WAY TO PENALIZE SOMEONE IS WITH SILLY STRING. IF SHE DECIDES TO BE THE FIRST ONE TO PASS OUT, BREAK OPEN THAT CASE OF SILLY STRING AND COVER HER ENTIRE BODY. SILLY STRING CAN REALLY MAKE A MESS, BUT IT ENCOURAGES SLEEPY INDIVIDUALS TO DO THEIR LAUNDRY, WHICH IS SOMETIMES PUT OFF A LITTLE TOO LONG IN SCHOOL.

ADDED BONUS: Carry a can of Silly String around campus and play the ultimate game of tag. You get extra points if you spray someone before class!

PRANK UNIVERSITY

035 UNDERWEAR SWITCH

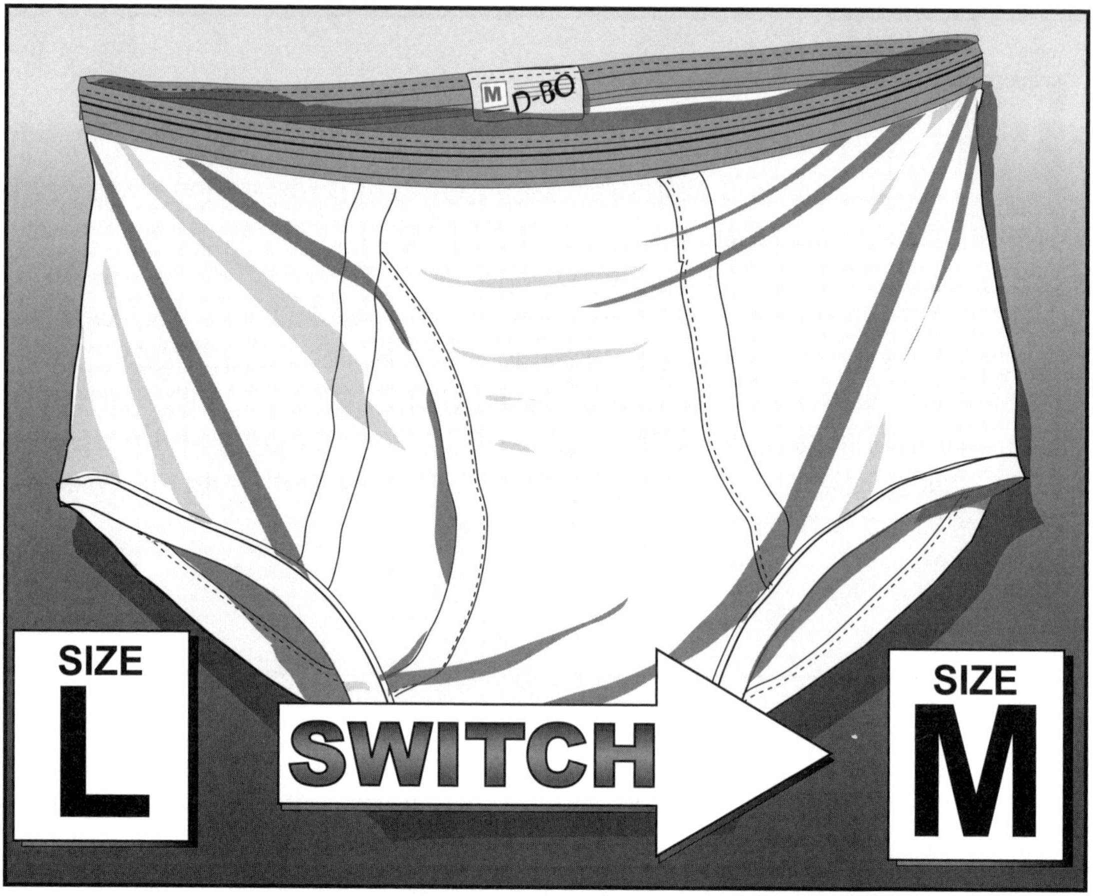

3

SUCCESSFUL ATTEMPTS

1	2	3	4	5	6	7	8	9	10	11	12	13	14	15	16	17

WEARING TOO-SMALL UNDERWEAR IS ONE OF THE MOST UNCOMFORTABLE FEELINGS IN THE WORLD. NEXT TIME YOUR ROOMMATE BUYS SOME NEW UNDERWEAR, GO TO THAT SAME STORE AND PURCHASE THE SAME DESIGN AND BRAND, BUT TWO SIZES TOO SMALL. REPLACE HIS UNDERWEAR WITH YOUR NEWLY PURCHASED EXTRA-TIGHT TIGHTY-WHITIES. IF YOU FEEL LIKE SAVING A FEW DOLLARS, JUST RUN ALL HIS UNDERWEAR IN THE DRYER FOR A DAY; IT SHOULD SHRINK, DEPENDING ON WHAT IT'S MADE OF. DON'T FORGET TO WRITE HIS NAME ON THE LABEL, JUST LIKE HIS MOM USED TO DO!

ADDED BONUS: Stain all his underwear with melted chocolate or yellow food coloring and leave it lying around his room. Girls really dig dirty underwear; he'll thank you.

PRANK UNIVERSITY

036 XXX SUBSCRIPTION

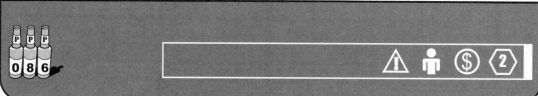

SUCCESSFUL ATTEMPTS

1	2	3	4	5	6	7	8	9	10	11	12	13	14	15	16	17

HONESTLY, SIGNING SOMEONE UP FOR SUBSCRIPTIONS TO NUDIE MAGAZINES *IS* A PRANK. IF YOUR ROOMMATE IS STARTING TO GET ON YOUR NERVES, FILL OUT ONE OF THOSE TRIAL OFFERS AND HAVE IT SENT TO HIS PARENTS' HOUSE. MAKE SURE HIS NAME IS ON IT. THIS WILL CERTAINLY MAKE FOR SOME INTERESTING SUNDAY-NIGHT PHONE CALLS FROM MOM. THE MORE TRIAL OFFERS THE BETTER—JUST MAKE SURE YOU EVENTUALLY CANCEL THEM OR HAVE THEM REDIRECTED TO YOU—YOU DON'T WANT GOOD READING MATERIAL GOING TO WASTE!

ADDED BONUS: If your roommate has just moved out of your place to bunk up with a girl, sign her up for *Playgirl* and watch the fun begin.

PRANK UNIVERSITY

037 PLASTIC FORKING

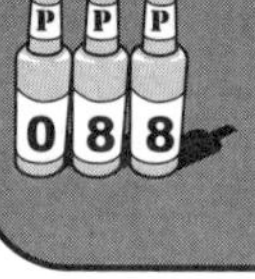

SUCCESSFUL ATTEMPTS

1	2	3	4	5	6	7	8	9	10	11	12	13	14	15	16	17

THIS ONE COULD ALSO BE CALLED "DIRTY KNEES." ONLY A FEW KNOW ABOUT THE ART OF A GOOD PLASTIC FORKING, BUT I'M WILLING TO SHARE IT HERE. THE TRICK IS TO USE AS MANY PLASTIC FORKS AS IS HUMANLY POSSIBLE. QUIETLY AND EVENLY SPACED, YOU'LL NEED TO STAB THE FORKS INTO YOUR VICTIM'S TURF. IF YOU BUY YOUR FORKS IN BULK, SIX HUNDRED FORKS WILL RUN YOU ABOUT TWENTY-TWO DOLLARS. FUN DOESN'T GET MUCH CHEAPER THAN THAT! IN ADDITION TO SOME CASH, YOU WILL NEED A FRIEND TO HELP YOU PULL THIS OFF. ANY UTENSIL CAN BE SUBSTITUTED.

ADDED BONUS: Use fertilizer or weed-killer to spell out the word "fork." That way your victim will remember the night of the six hundred plastic forks for at least a few months.

PRANK UNIVERSITY

038 WET BED

SUCCESSFUL ATTEMPTS

1	2	3	4	5	6	7	8	9	10	11	12	13	14	15	16	17

IF YOU CAN'T TAKE AN ANNOYING HOUSEMATE ANYMORE, THIS IS YOUR LAST RESORT. GO INTO YOUR VICTIM'S ROOM AND POUR WATER IN HIS BED. THEN COVER IT BACK UP WITH THE BLANKET. COMING HOME TIRED AND ALONE, HE WILL TURN OFF THE LIGHTS AND JUMP IN BED, ONLY TO FIND A HUGE PUDDLE OF WATER. THIS WILL REALLY UPSET HIM, AND HE WILL PROBABLY WAKE UP EVERYONE IN THE HOUSE. REMEMBER, THIS PRANK IS A LAST RESORT; YOU NEED YOUR SLEEP, TOO.

ADDED BONUS: If your roommate has a waterbed, poor a cup of water on one corner every day for a week—convince him the bed has a leak!

PRANK UNIVERSITY

039 ALL TIED UP

SUCCESSFUL ATTEMPTS

1	2	3	4	5	6	7	8	9	10	11	12	13	14	15	16	17

HERE IS ONE OF THE OLDEST TRICKS IN THE BOOK, TAKEN TO A WHOLE NEW LEVEL. TIE YOUR POOR ROOMMATE'S SHOES TOGETHER WHEN HE'S NOT LOOKING. SURE, THIS IS CHILDISH, BUT ISN'T THAT THE POINT? THINK ABOUT IT: THE NIGHT BEFORE A BIG TEST, YOU SNEAK INTO YOUR ROOMMATE'S CLOSET AND TIE ALL OF HIS SHOES TOGETHER, EXCEPT FOR HIS WINTER BOOTS, USING DOUBLE AND TRIPLE KNOTS. IN THE MORNING WHEN HE'S JUST ABOUT TO GO TO CLASS, HE PICKS UP A SNARL OF SHOES! WITH NO TIME TO WASTE, HE'LL HAVE TO JUMP INTO HIS BOOTS!

ADDED BONUS: Another quick solution is to remove all the laces in his shoes. He'll be wearing flip-flops till the end of the year.

PRANK UNIVERSITY

040 GAY PORN SCREEN SAVER

SUCCESSFUL ATTEMPTS

1	2	3	4	5	6	7	8	9	10	11	12	13	14	15	16	17

ON YOUR ROOMMATE'S PARENTS' NEXT VISIT TO YOUR PATHETIC HOUSE, HAVE A LITTLE SURPRISE WAITING FOR THEM. RIGHT BEFORE HIS PARENTS ENTER THE ROOM, CHANGE YOUR ROOMMATE'S DESKTOP IMAGE ON HIS PC TO SOMETHING VULGAR. YOU CAN ALSO DOWNLOAD SOME REALLY INTERESTING SCREEN SAVERS. IF YOUR ROOMMATE IS OUT OF THE CLOSET, THROW THE OPPOSITE SEX ON THE COMPUTER; REALLY MESS WITH HIS POOR DAD'S HEAD! REMEMBER, THIS PRANK CAN ALSO BE EXECUTED FOR OTHER VISITORS TO THE HOUSE, NOT JUST MOM AND DAD.

ADDED BONUS: Squirt some white hand lotion on the keyboard. Less is more!

PRANK UNIVERSITY

041 CAR FOR SALE

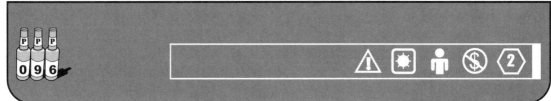

SUCCESSFUL ATTEMPTS

1	2	3	4	5	6	7	8	9	10	11	12	13	14	15	16	17

IF YOUR ROOMMATE DECIDES TO FLY HOME TO VISIT HIS PARENTS FOR THE WEEKEND, HAVE A LITTLE YARD SALE ON HIS BEHALF. PUT HIS MOTORCYCLE OR CAR ON THE FRONT LAWN WITH A "FOR SALE" SIGN ON IT. MAKE SURE YOU PUT HIS MOBILE-PHONE NUMBER ON THE SIGN, ALONG WITH A VERY LOW PRICE, SO HE RECEIVES A TON OF CALLS. HE'LL BE VISITING THE FOLKS WITH HIS PHONE RINGING OFF THE HOOK! HE'LL BE FORCED TO EXPLAIN TO TOTAL STRANGERS THAT HIS CAR OR MOTORCYCLE IS NOT FOR SALE. WHO KNOWS, HE MIGHT GET SOME REALLY GOOD OFFERS AND DECIDE TO SELL IT AFTER ALL. THE ONLY MONEY YOU WILL HAVE TO SPEND ON THIS PRANK IS BUYING THE SIGN, UNLESS YOU CAN JUST MAKE ONE.

ADDED BONUS: Another eye-catching sign is: "24-Year-Old Virgin for Sale."

PRANK UNIVERSITY

042 ROPE LOCK

SUCCESSFUL ATTEMPTS

1	2	3	4	5	6	7	8	9	10	11	12	13	14	15	16	17

MAKING THE DRUNKEN WALK HOME CAN BE SOMEWHAT BORING AT 2:30 IN THE MORNING. IF YOU HAVE AN OUNCE OF ENERGY, ROUND UP ABOUT TEN FEET OF ROPE AND GO VISIT YOUR BUDDIES! THE EARLY HOURS OF THE MORNING, AFTER THE BARS CLOSE, WILL GIVE YOU PLENTY OF TIME TO TIE ALL YOUR FRIENDS' DOORS SHUT. YOU MAY HAVE TO OPEN THE SCREEN DOOR TO GET TO THE MAIN DOOR, SO BE SURE TO BE QUIET! MAKE SURE THAT THE ROPE IS TIGHT AND TIED TO A STURDY OBJECT LIKE A BANISTER OR EVEN THE MAILBOX. YOUR BUDDIES WILL EVENTUALLY HAVE TO CRAWL OUT THEIR WINDOWS OR CALL A FRIEND—MAYBE EVEN YOU—TO LET THEM OUT. THIS PRANK SHOULD ONLY BE PLAYED ON COLLEGE FRIENDS; ELDERLY PEOPLE HAVE A TOUGH TIME CLIMBING OUT OF WINDOWS.

ADDED BONUS: You can also make this work in the dorms; simply tie one door to another.

PRANK UNIVERSITY

043 PARKING BRAKES

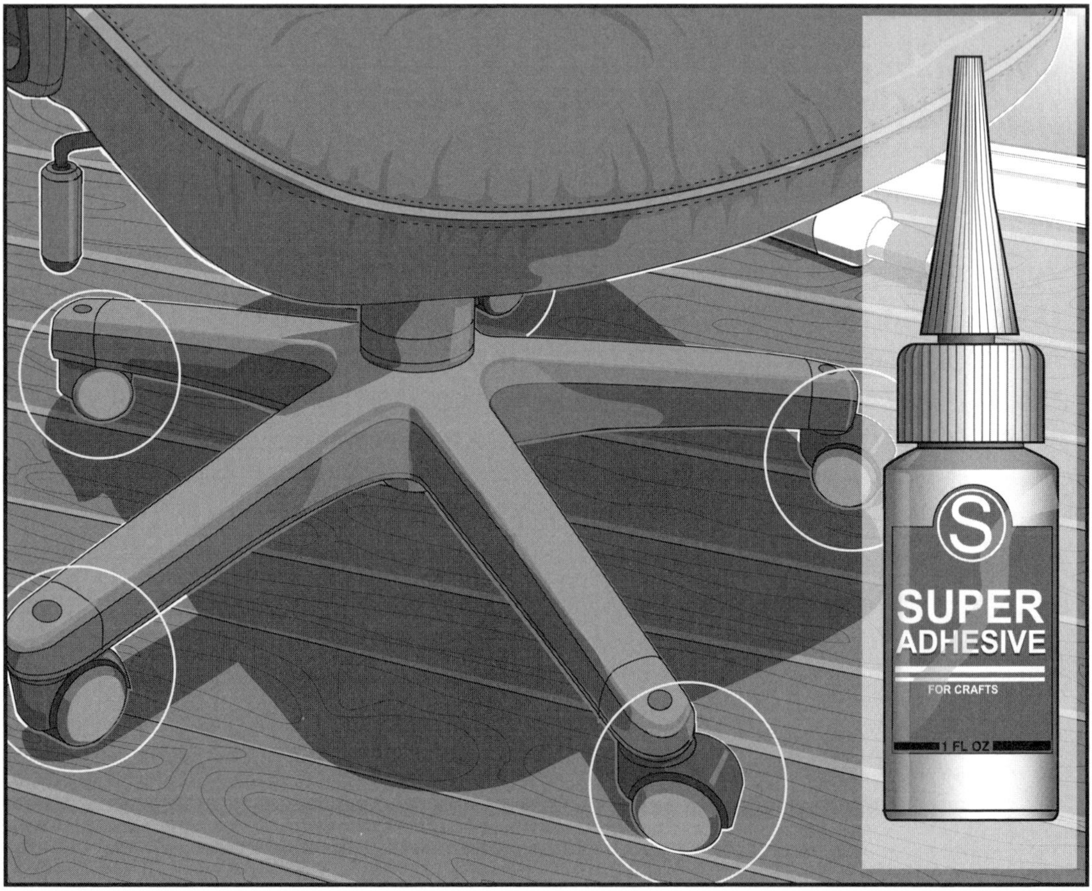

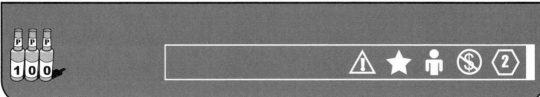

SUCCESSFUL ATTEMPTS

1	2	3	4	5	6	7	8	9	10	11	12	13	14	15	16	17

IF YOU CAN'T STAND THE SOUND OF YOUR ROOMMATE'S ROLLING DESK CHAIR, GLUE THE WHEELS! THE NEXT TIME HE JUMPS ON HIS CHAIR AND TRIES TO ROLL BACK, HE'LL FALL BACKWARD INSTEAD. IF YOU WANT TO PROLONG THE PROCESS, GLUE ONE WHEEL PER WEEK. HE'LL BE REALLY CONFUSED AND ANNOYED. HE'LL PROBABLY PISS AND MOAN ABOUT HIS THIRTY-DOLLAR OFFICE CHAIR, TOO. JUST REMEMBER THAT SOME OFFICE CHAIRS CAN COST AS MUCH AS EIGHT HUNDRED DOLLARS, SO BE CAREFUL NOT TO MESS WITH THOSE—IT MAY COST YOU *MUCHO DINERO.*

ADDED BONUS: Cover the wheels in black shoe polish, and "follow those tracks."

PRANK UNIVERSITY

044 QUICK TWO-STEPPER

SUCCESSFUL ATTEMPTS

1	2	3	4	5	6	7	8	9	10	11	12	13	14	15	16	17

THE NAME SAYS IT ALL: THE "QUICK TWO-STEPPER." YOU WILL FIRST HAVE TO LOCK YOUR ROOMMATE IN HIS OWN ROOM. ONCE THAT IS ACCOMPLISHED, AND HE DECIDES NOT TO BREAK THE DOOR DOWN, HE WILL GO FOR THE WINDOW. MAKE SURE YOU ARE ABOVE THAT WINDOW, WAITING. YOU MAY HAVE TO RUN TO THE NEXT FLOOR, OR EVEN GET ON THE ROOF. HAVE A LARGE PAIL OF WATER AT HAND. SURE, WATER ISN'T SO BAD, BUT IF HE IS TRYING TO GO TO CLASS, HE WILL WANT TO AVOID IT AT ALL COSTS. AS SOON AS YOU SEE HIS HEAD, START POURING.

ADDED BONUS: Basement roommates usually have tiny windows. Throw a nice-sized smoke bomb outside that window.

PRANK UNIVERSITY

045 LIGHTS OUT IN CHINATOWN

SUCCESSFUL ATTEMPTS

1	2	3	4	5	6	7	8	9	10	11	12	13	14	15	16	17

LIGHTS OUT IN CHINATOWN!" YOUR ROOMMATE HAS JUST CLOSED THE BATHROOM DOOR. YOU HAVE ONE OF TWO OPTIONS: FIRST, LET HIM DO HIS BUSINESS IN PEACE; SECOND, MESS WITH HIM! RUN DOWNSTAIRS AND FIND THE POWER BOX, LOCATE THE SWITCH FOR THE BATHROOM, THEN PULL THE BREAKER. IF YOU ARE UNABLE TO LOCATE THE RIGHT SWITCH, JUST FLIP THEM ALL. REMEMBER, YOUR PC WILL ALSO TURN OFF, SO SAVE ANY WORK YOU NEED BEFORE YOU START FLIPPING SWITCHES ON YOUR BITCHES. AS FOR YOUR ROOMMATE, HE'LL BE SITTING IN COMPLETE DARKNESS. SITTING ON THE TOILET IN THE PITCH-DARK CAN CAUSE SOME UNPLEASANT COMPLICATIONS, ESPECIALLY IF YOU REMOVE THE TOILET PAPER BEFORE HE GOES IN THERE.

ADDED BONUS: If he's taking a shower, slide a bunch of upside-down bottle caps under the door. Bare feet meet pointy bottle caps—ouch.

PRANK UNIVERSITY

046 SLEEPY PEDICURE

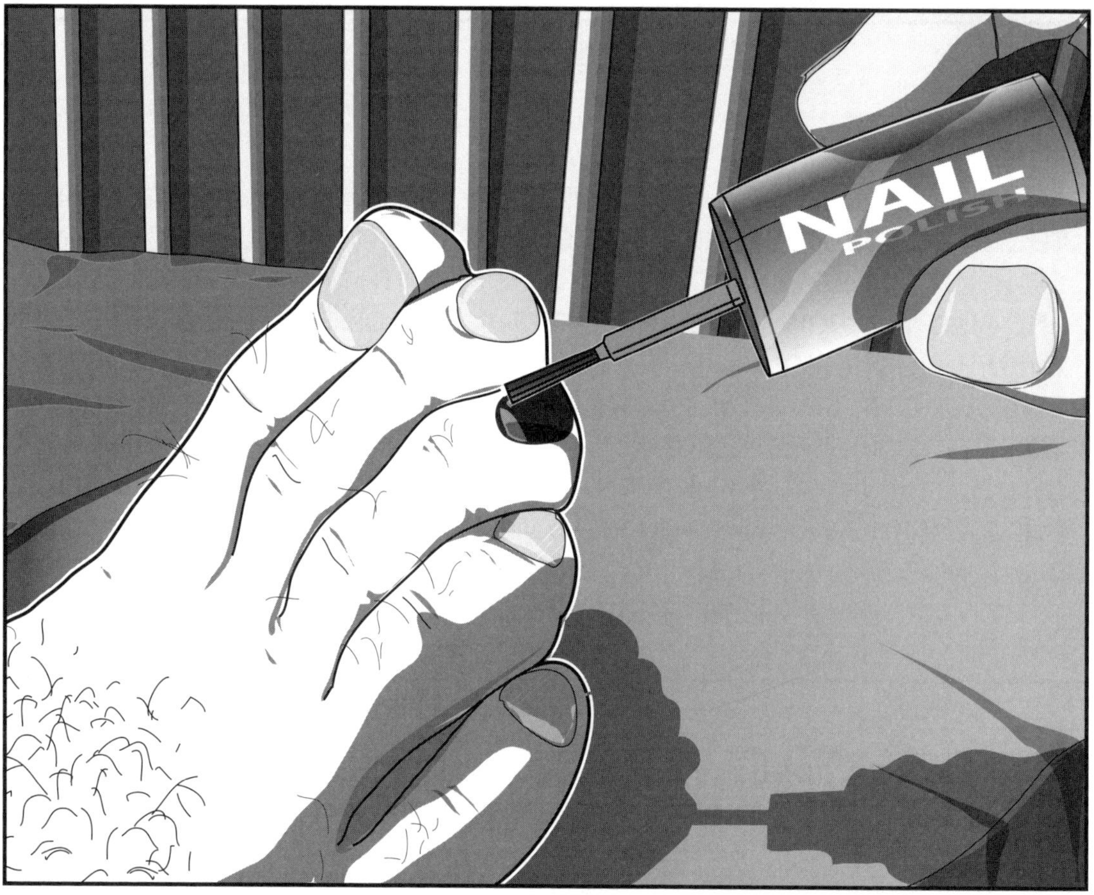

106

SUCCESSFUL ATTEMPTS

1	2	3	4	5	6	7	8	9	10	11	12	13	14	15	16	17

GUYS LOOK GOOD WITH PAINTED NAILS! NO, REALLY; AFTER YOUR BUDDY HAS PASSED OUT ON YOUR SOFA, REMOVE HIS SHOES AND SOCKS AND GET TO WORK. ONCE YOUR WORK IS DONE, WAIT A FEW MINUTES TO LET THE PAINT DRY. NOW, PUT HIS STINKY-ASS SOCKS AND SHOES BACK ON, LIKE NOTHING EVER HAPPENED. THIS WORKS BEST IN SUMMER, SINCE TOES COME OUT AND VISIT MORE OFTEN THEN. IF YOU HAVE TIME, DO HIS FINGERS, TOO. DON'T FORGET THE PHOTOS, OF COURSE.

ADDED BONUS: A touch of eye shadow wouldn't hurt, either. A dress may be pushing it, but you get three bonus points if you can pull that off.

PRANK UNIVERSITY

047 DORM EVICTION

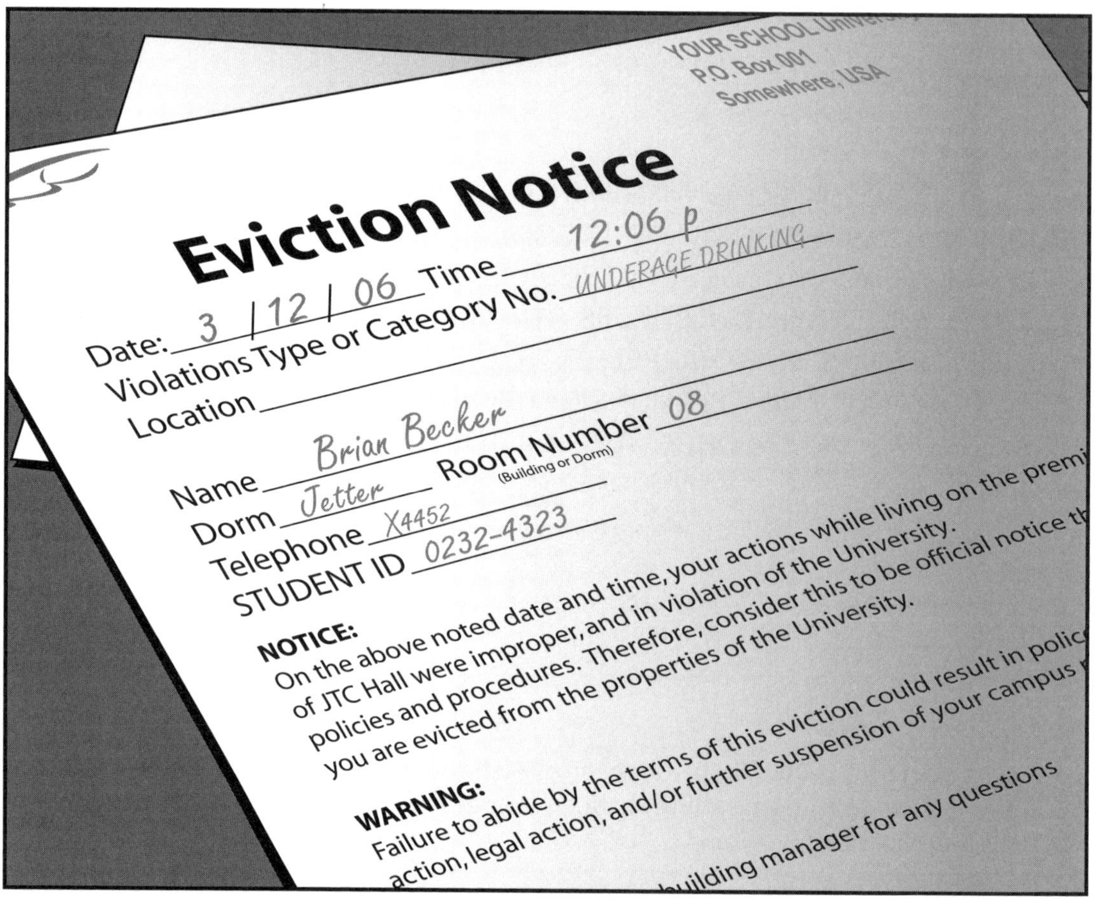

YOUR SCHOOL University
P.O. Box 001
Somewhere, USA
Eviction Notice
Date: 3 / 12 / 06 Time 12:06 p
Violations Type or Category No. UNDERAGE DRINKING
Location
Name Brian Becker Room Number 08
(Building or Dorm)
Dorm Jetter
Telephone X4452
STUDENT ID 0232-4323
NOTICE:
On the above noted date and time, your actions while living on the premi
of JTC Hall were improper, and in violation of the University.
policies and procedures. Therefore, consider this to be official notice th
you are evicted from the properties of the University.
WARNING:
Failure to abide by the terms of this eviction could result in polic
action, legal action, and/or further suspension of your campus r
building manager for any questions

SUCCESSFUL ATTEMPTS

1	2	3	4	5	6	7	8	9	10	11	12	13	14	15	16	17

THROUGHOUT THE COURSE OF THE YEAR, YOU WILL RECEIVE ALL KINDS OF MAILINGS FROM YOUR SCHOOL. SOMETIMES THE UNIVERSITY AFFAIRS OFFICE DOESN'T BOTHER SEALING AN ENVELOPE. KEEP THESE, AS THEY WILL COME IN HANDY. OR, IF MAILINGS ARE IN SHORT SUPPLY, MOST CAMPUS STATIONERY CAN BE RE-CREATED ON YOUR COMPUTER. WRITE UP A FAKE EVICTION NOTICE, INFORMING ONE OF YOUR FRIENDS THAT HIS ON-CAMPUS CONTRACT HAS BEEN TERMINATED. GIVE HIM THE OPTION TO MAKE AN APPOINTMENT WITH THE RESIDENTIAL ADVISOR, OR EVEN THE DEAN. YOU GET THREE BONUS POINTS IF HE OR SHE SETS UP A MEETING WITH THE DEAN, AND GOES.

ADDED BONUS: You can also write up a car decree for on-campus parking locations due to complaints.

PRANK UNIVERSITY

048 HIBERNATION

SUCCESSFUL ATTEMPTS

1	2	3	4	5	6	7	8	9	10	11	12	13	14	15	16	17

HIBERNATION IS SPENDING PART OF THE COLD SEASON IN A MORE OR LESS DORMANT STATE, APPARENTLY AS PROTECTION FROM COLD WHEN NORMAL BODY TEMPERATURE CANNOT BE MAINTAINED AND FOOD IS SCARCE. THAT SURE SOUNDS LIKE COLLEGE TO ME! SOME PEOPLE ONLY WAKE UP WHEN IT GETS LIGHT OUT. HOPEFULLY YOU LIVE WITH ONE OF THOSE PEOPLE! LATE ONE NIGHT, WHEN YOUR ROOMMATE IS ALL NESTLED IN BED, COVER ALL HIS WINDOWS IN CARDBOARD AND BLACK PLASTIC BAGS. YOU SHOULD USE INDUSTRIAL PACKING TAPE; OTHERWISE, HE MIGHT HEAR YOUR HAMMER. IN THE DARKNESS THE POOR GUY WILL THINK IT'S SIX IN THE MORNING, AND JUST KEEP SLEEPING. DON'T FORGET THE TOWEL UNDER THE DOOR TO BLOCK ANY AND ALL LIGHT.

ADDED BONUS: Combine this prank with Prank #93, “Early Shower” but reverse his clock so that twelve your time is only six his time.

PRANK UNIVERSITY

049 BEER-BOTTLE BED

SUCCESSFUL ATTEMPTS

1	2	3	4	5	6	7	8	9	10	11	12	13	14	15	16	17

YOUR ROOMMATE HAS JUST FALLEN ASLEEP FOR THE NIGHT. ROUND UP YOUR OTHER ROOMMATES AND FOUR EMPTY BEER BOTTLES. TWO GUYS WILL NEED TO SLOWLY LIFT THE BED AS YOU SLIP A BEER BOTTLE UNDER EACH POST. YOUR ROOMMATES WILL NEED TO HOLD THE BED AS STEADY AS THEY CAN. HAVE THEM SLOWLY LOWER THE BED UNTIL IT RESTS ON THE BEER BOTTLES, WITHOUT KNOCKING THEM OVER. NOW, JUST LEAVE THE ROOM AND LET HIM TOSS AND TURN TILL HIS BED FALLS DOWN WITH A CRASH.

ADDED BONUS: Everyone leave the room except for the cameraman. Now, someone else, start pounding on the door! Film that fool jumping up, and then falling down.

PRANK UNIVERSITY

050 SLEEPOVER

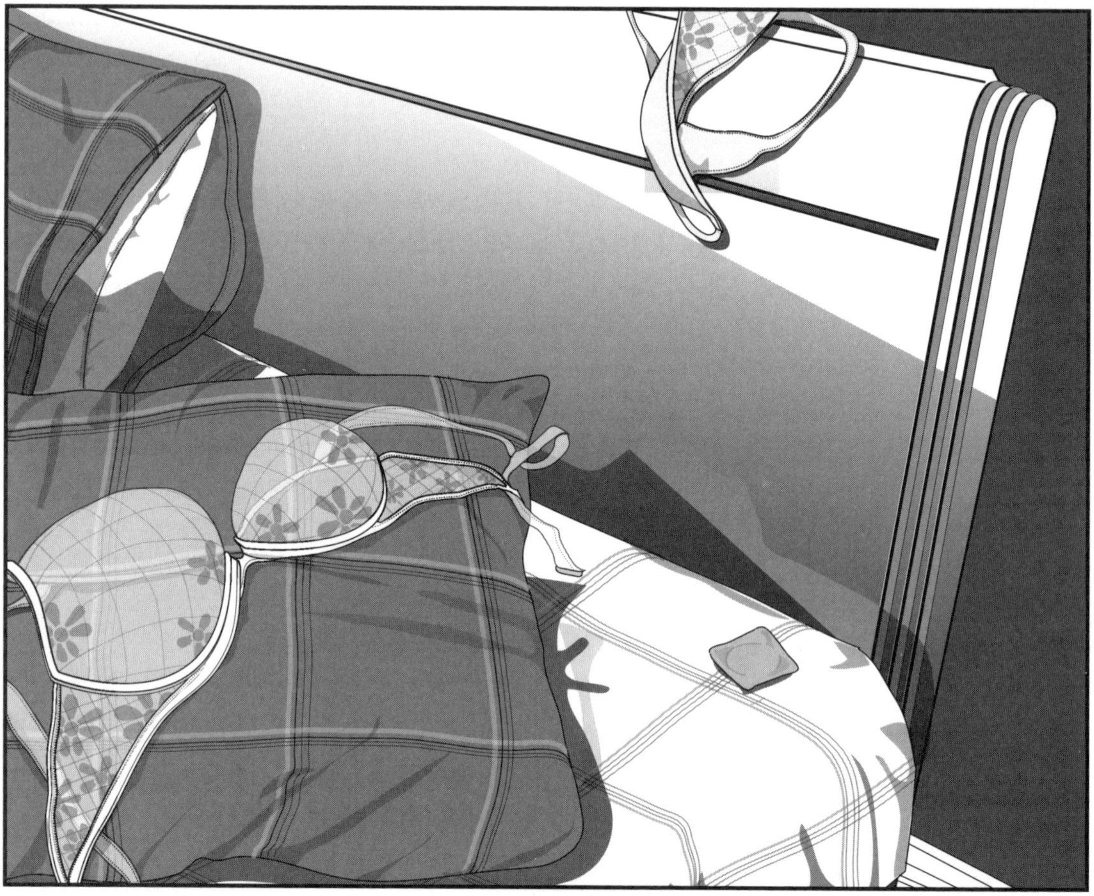

									SUCCESSFUL ATTEMPTS							
1	2	3	4	5	6	7	8	9	10	11	12	13	14	15	16	17

IN COLLEGE, YOU WILL OFTEN FIND THAT YOU AND YOUR ROOMMATES SHARE EVERYTHING. BUT THE LAST THING YOU WANT IS TO SHARE YOUR BED. IF YOUR ROOMMATE IS GONE FOR THE NIGHT, MAKE IT LOOK LIKE YOU BROUGHT SOMEONE HOME LAST NIGHT, TO HIS ROOM. UNMAKE HIS BED, MESS IT ALL UP, AND LEAVE A FOREIGN PAIR OF UNDERWEAR INSIDE THE SHEETS. YOU CAN ALSO ADD EXTRA TOUCHES, LIKE A BRA, WHIPPED CREAM, OR SOME KIND OF CONTRACEPTIVE. IT ALSO HELPS IF YOU SPRAY SOME PERFUME OR COLOGNE ON THE SHEETS. YOUR ROOMMATE WILL COME HOME AND FIND OUT THAT SOMEONE HAS BEEN SLEEPING IN HIS BED!

ADDED BONUS: Leave someone's phone number on the nightstand; your roommate will want to do some detective work to figure this out. If you can locate his ex-girlfriend's phone number, leave that one on the nightstand for bonus points.

PRANK UNIVERSITY

051 BANANA IN THE TAILPIPE

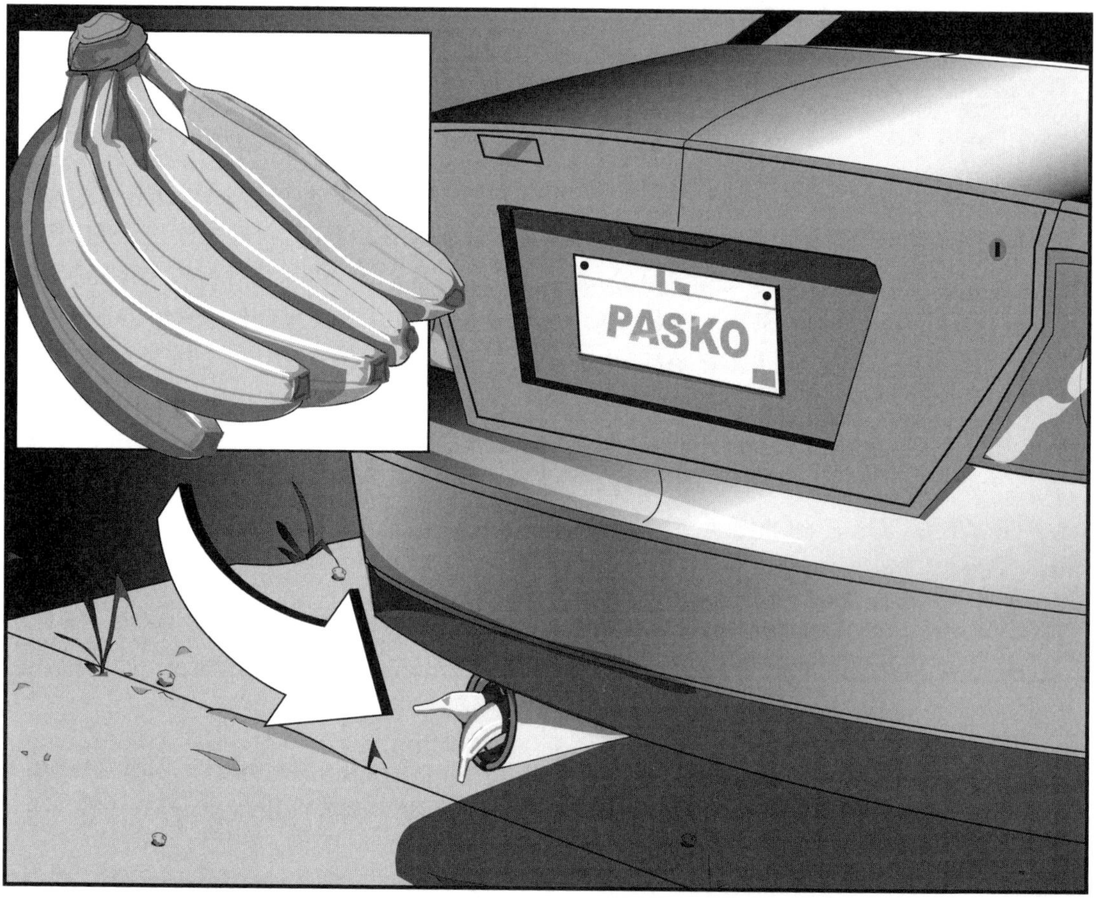

SUCCESSFUL ATTEMPTS

1	2	3	4	5	6	7	8	9	10	11	12	13	14	15	16	17

IF YOU PLUG YOUR ROOMMATE'S EXHAUST PIPE WITH A BUNCH OF BANANAS, HIS CAR WILL BEHAVE LIKE IT'S NOT RECEIVING ENOUGH FUEL. THE DRIVER WILL ALSO HAVE A TOUGH TIME ACCELERATING. IF YOU PACK THE BANANAS IN THERE REAL GOOD, THE CAR COULD ALSO "CUT OUT" WHILE YOUR ROOMMATE IS DRIVING. BUT MAKE SURE YOU CONFESS BEFORE YOUR ROOMMATE TAKES THE CAR TO THE SHOP; THE COST OF TAKING A CAR TO A MECHANIC CAN BE ASTRONOMICAL.

ADDED BONUS: Place a large balloon or condom around the exhaust pipe. When he starts up the car, it will inflate, and then explode!

PRANK UNIVERSITY

052 EGG'N

SUCCESSFUL ATTEMPTS

1 | 2 | 3 | 4 | 5 | 6 | 7 | 8 | 9 | 10 | 11 | 12 | 13 | 14 | 15 | 16 | 17

THIS IS A QUICK AND EASY WAY TO GET EVEN WITH SOMEONE. ONE CHEAP CARTON OF EGGS WILL DO IT. LAUNCH THEM AT THE HOUSE FROM AS FAR AWAY AS POSSIBLE, SO YOU HAVE A GOOD DISTANCE BETWEEN YOU AND ANYONE WHO COMES RUNNING OUT. YOU COULD END UP WITH A LARGE FINE IF SOMEONE CATCHES YOU, AND THEY'LL PROBABLY MAKE YOU CLEAN THEIR HOUSE TO BOOT. IF YOU ARE ON THE RECEIVING END OF THIS PRANK, YOU'LL HATE LIFE; CLEANING EGGS OFF YOUR HOUSE IS ONE OF THE WORST WAYS TO SPEND A SATURDAY MORNING.

ADDED BONUS: Unscrew your neighbor's back porch light and place a bunch of unbroken eggs on the steps.

PRANK UNIVERSITY

053 DOOR REMOVAL

SUCCESSFUL ATTEMPTS

1	2	3	4	5	6	7	8	9	10	11	12	13	14	15	16	17

LATE ONE NIGHT IN DORM LAND, SNEAK UP TO THE FLOOR ABOVE YOURS AND UNSCREW AND REMOVE ALL THE DOORS ON THE BATHROOM STALLS. NOW, WITHOUT BEING SEEN, RUN DOWN TO YOUR FLOOR. YOU CAN HIDE THE DOORS IN ONE OF TWO SPOTS: UNDERNEATH YOUR MATTRESS OR IN YOUR CLOSET, BEHIND YOUR CLOTHES. MOST LIKELY SOMEONE WILL WAKE UP AND HAVE TO USE THE RESTROOM BEFORE THE JANITORS ARRIVE. IT IS VERY UNCOMFORTABLE USING THE RESTROOM WHILE SOMEONE IS WATCHING. IF SOMEONE SPOTS YOU, ABORT THE MISSION, PUT DOWN THE DOORS, AND RUN. BUT BE SMART ABOUT IT—DON'T RUN FOR YOUR ROOM.

ADDED BONUS: Combine this with Prank #60, "Seat Less Thrown," for a real morning treat!

PRANK UNIVERSITY

054 BUMPER ART

SUCCESSFUL ATTEMPTS

1	2	3	4	5	6	7	8	9	10	11	12	13	14	15	16	17

SOME PEOPLE LOVE TO PUT STICKERS ON THE BACKS OF THEIR CARS. YOU KNOW THEM—STUPID PHRASES LIKE "ASPHALT EATER" OR "I'M A BITCH." OTHERS ENJOY BUMPER STICKERS FROM A DISTANCE, BUT WOULD NEVER DARE LITTER THEIR CARS WITH SUCH SILLY PROPAGANDA. GO OUT AND BUY A BUNCH OF OFFENSIVE STICKERS AND PLACE THEM ON YOUR FRIEND'S CAR. HE COULD GO WEEKS WITHOUT NOTICING. THE "HONK IF YOU CARE" STICKERS ARE YOUR BEST BET; TOTAL STRANGERS WILL BE HONKING AT YOUR ROOMMATE FOR NO REASON. HE WILL PROBABLY THINK THEY ARE INSULTING HIS DRIVING AND EXCHANGE SOME KIND OF BODY LANGUAGE—BONUS!

ADDED BONUS: Place a bunch of "Just Married" signs on random cars in the student parking lot. Also, a republican sticker on a democrat's car is like oil and water—they just don't mix.

PRANK UNIVERSITY

055 WASABI PASTE

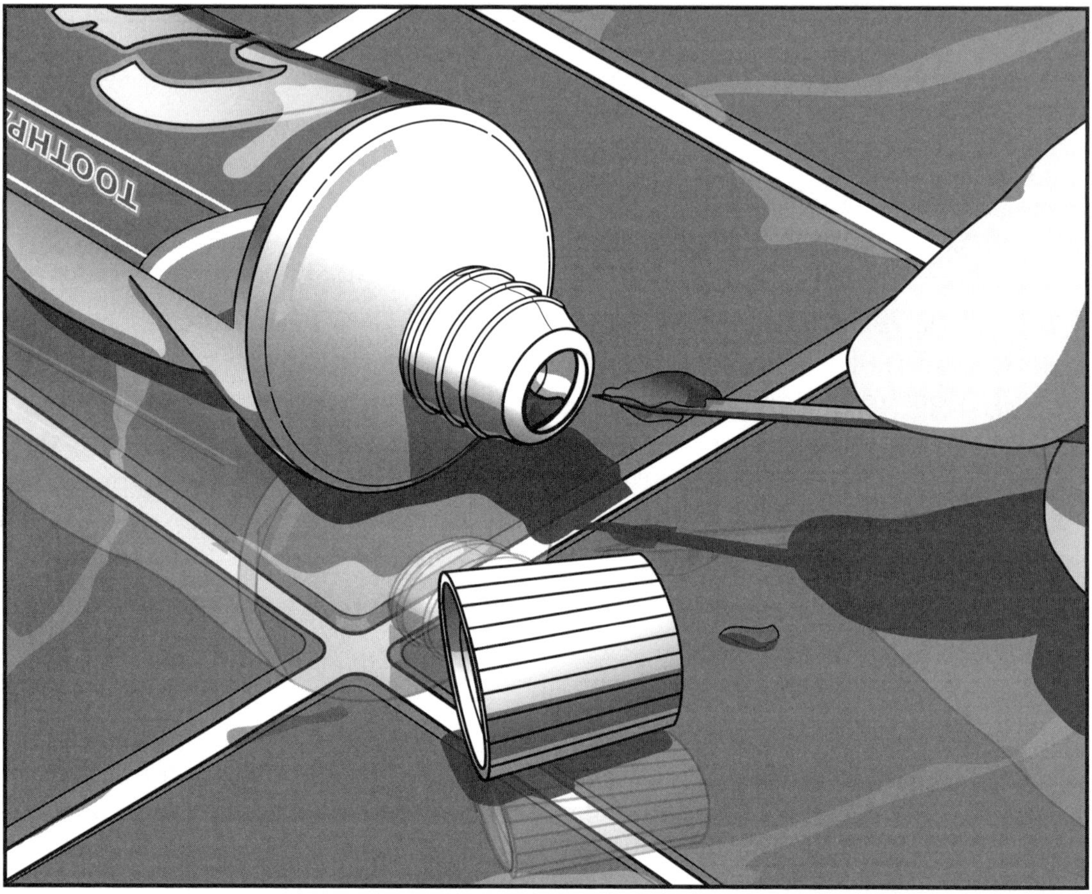

									SUCCESSFUL ATTEMPTS							
1	2	3	4	5	6	7	8	9	10	11	12	13	14	15	16	17

WASABI IS USUALLY SERVED WITH DISHES CONTAINING RAW FISH, POPULAR IN JAPAN AND RAPIDLY GROWING IN POPULARITY IN THE UNITED STATES. IT'S A JAPANESE DIP THAT KICKS LIKE A MULE—THAT IS, YOU'RE A JACKASS IF YOU EAT TOO MUCH! YOU MUST FIRST GO OUT AND LOCATE A SMALL CONTAINER OF WASABI TO COMPLETE THIS PRANK. NOW, WITH TOOTHPICK IN HAND, SCOOP UP SOME WASABI AND MIX IT INTO THE TOOTHPASTE TUBE. DON'T GO TOO FAR IN OR YOU'LL DILUTE THE POWER OF THE WASABI. WASABI IS GREEN, AS IS MINT TOOTHPASTE, SO THE BLENDING WON'T BE HARD. IF YOUR ROOMMATE STILL USES TRADITIONAL WHITE TOOTHPASTE, IT'S GOING TO BE A LITTLE HARDER TO PULL THIS PRANK OFF, BUT IN THAT CASE YOU CAN USE HORSERADISH, WHICH IS WHITE.

ADDED BONUS: Wasabi is hot as hell, so feel free to add it to any of your roommate's favorite dishes.

PRANK UNIVERSITY

056 ARTIFICIAL SALE

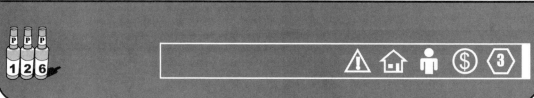

SUCCESSFUL ATTEMPTS

1	2	3	4	5	6	7	8	9	10	11	12	13	14	15	16	17

FAKE GARAGE SALES ARE A GREAT WAY TO MEET YOUR NEIGHBORS. THE DAY BEFORE, GO AROUND TOWN AND PLACE GARAGE-SALE SIGNS ALL OVER THE NEIGHBORHOOD. EARLY THE NEXT MORNING, PLACE ONE ON THE CORNER OF YOUR FRIENDS' LOT. THEY WILL HAVE ALL TYPES OF PEOPLE WALKING UP, LOOKING FOR GREAT BARGAINS, ONLY TO BE DISAPPOINTED. YOU MIGHT ALSO WANT TO PLACE AN AD IN THE PAPER. THE MORE PEOPLE THE BETTER. GOOD LUCK!

ADDED BONUS: Post signs around campus for an upcoming celebrity visit. Make sure you have all the necessary info on the sign so it's completely believable. This prank could possibly get you in the school newspaper, which is a great honor.

PRANK UNIVERSITY

057 CLEANUP

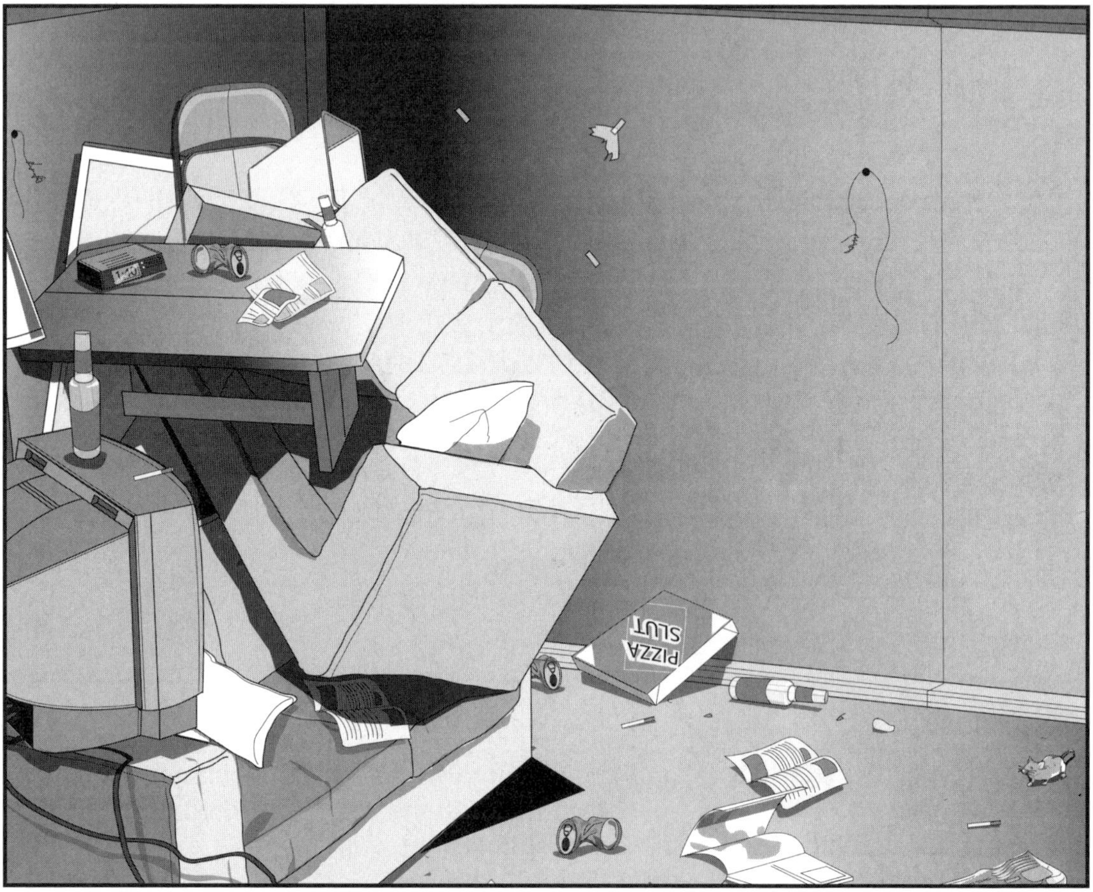

SUCCESSFUL ATTEMPTS

1	2	3	4	5	6	7	8	9	10	11	12	13	14	15	16	17

ROUND UP SOME FRIENDS AND GO PAY YOUR BUDDY A VISIT. TAKE EVERYTHING YOU CAN AND PILE IT UP IN THE BACK OF HIS ROOM—MAKE IT LOOK LIKE AN EARTHQUAKE HIT! THIS WILL ONLY TAKE A FEW MINUTES. YOU CAN PROBABLY EVEN PULL IT OFF WHEN YOUR NEIGHBOR RUNS TO THE SHOWER, BUT YOU'LL HAVE TO MOVE FAST AND HAVE A GOOD WORKING CREW WITH YOU. MAKE SURE YOU MOVE EVERYTHING, EVEN THE MAGAZINES, TRASH, AND PIZZA BOXES. HELPING AROUND THE HOUSE IS ALWAYS APPRECIATED.

ADDED BONUS: Once everything is in place, tie it all together, or cover it with industrial wrap (see Prank #14, "Industrial Auto Wrap").

PRANK UNIVERSITY

058 FAKE FRAT LETTERS

SUCCESSFUL ATTEMPTS

1	2	3	4	5	6	7	8	9	10	11	12	13	14	15	16	17

IF YOU AND YOUR NON-FRAT BUDDIES ARE LOOKING FOR A FUN PROJECT THIS SEMESTER, START A FRAT WAR. BASICALLY, YOU PICK TWO FRATS ON CAMPUS AND TARGET THEM FOR THE SEMESTER. CUT OUT ONE SET OF GREEK LETTERS AND PLACE THEM IN FRONT OF THE OTHER'S HOUSE. THIS WILL ENRAGE THAT HOUSE, AND THEY WILL PLAN AN ATTACK ON THE OTHER HOUSE. WARNING: THOSE FRAT HOUSES ARE LIKE BEE-HIVES; A WORLD OF HURT COMES BUZZING OUT OF THEM IF THEY CATCH YOU. REMEMBER, YOU ONLY HAVE TO START THE WAR; YOU DON'T HAVE TO FINISH IT. IF YOU'RE LOOKING TO DECORATE YOUR OWN COLLEGE HOUSE WITH GREEK LETTERS, YOU SHOULD GO WITH THE POPULAR NAME "I TAP-A KEG-A." IT IS AN INTERNATIONALLY RECOGNIZED FRATERNITY!

ADDED BONUS: If you have a special vendetta, "D.I.C." is a great logo to plaster on someone's fraternity house.

PRANK UNIVERSITY

059 WATER CUSHION

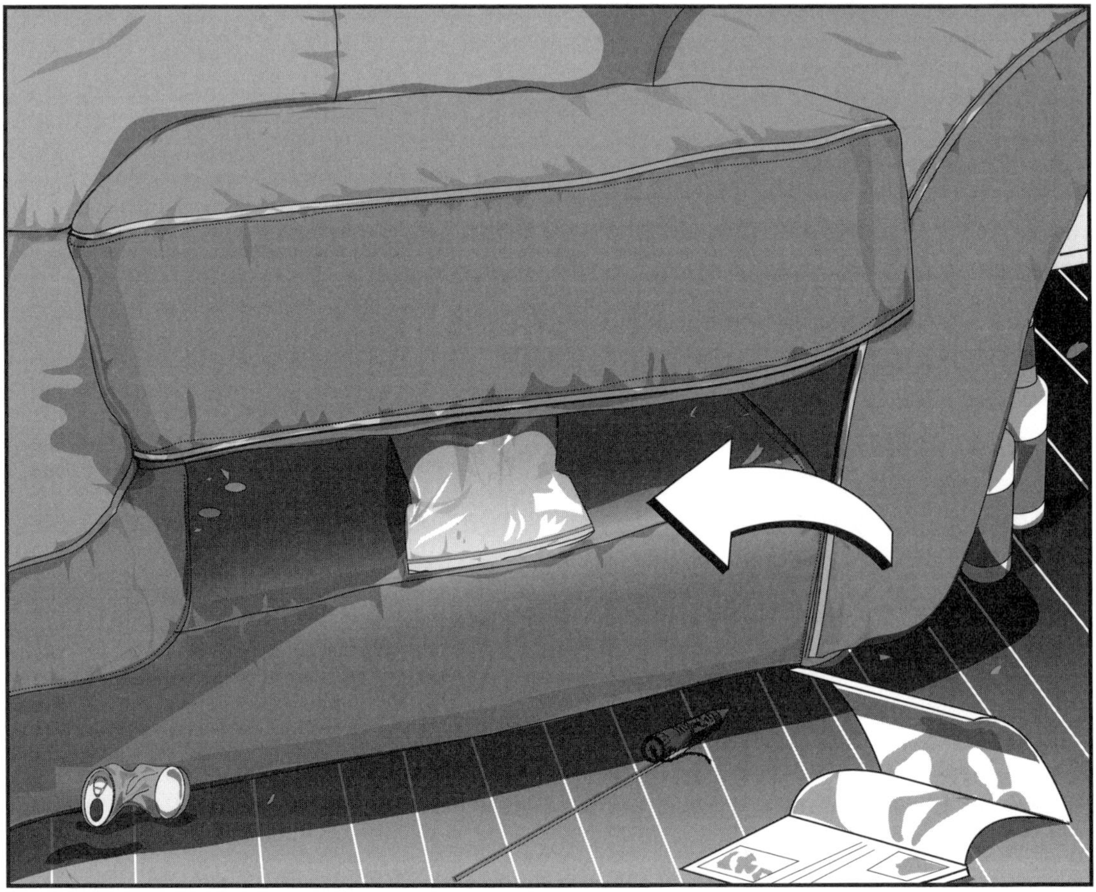

SUCCESSFUL ATTEMPTS

1	2	3	4	5	6	7	8	9	10	11	12	13	14	15	16	17

FILL A FREEZER BAG FULL OF WATER AND SEAL IT LIGHTLY. NOW, PLACE THE FILLED FREEZER BAG UNDER YOUR FRIEND'S SOFA CUSHION. THE SEAL SHOULD BE LOCATED TOWARD THE EDGE OF THE SOFA. WHEN YOUR FRIEND DECIDES TO SIT DOWN FOR A QUICK VIDEO GAME, HE'LL HAVE NIAGARA FALLS BETWEEN HIS LEGS. NOT ONLY WILL HE BE REALLY PISSED, BUT THE SOFA WILL BE WET FOR DAYS. THIS TRICK CAN ALSO BE USED UNDER CHAIR CUSHIONS, OR EVEN IN BED. YOU CAN ALSO FILL THE FREEZER BAG WITH WHIPPED CREAM—JUST DON'T SEAL IT.

ADDED BONUS: Placing a dead squirrel or mouse under someone's cushion can really make a statement. Depending on their cleaning habits, they will probably locate the carcass within a month.

PRANK UNIVERSITY

060 SEAT LESS THROWN

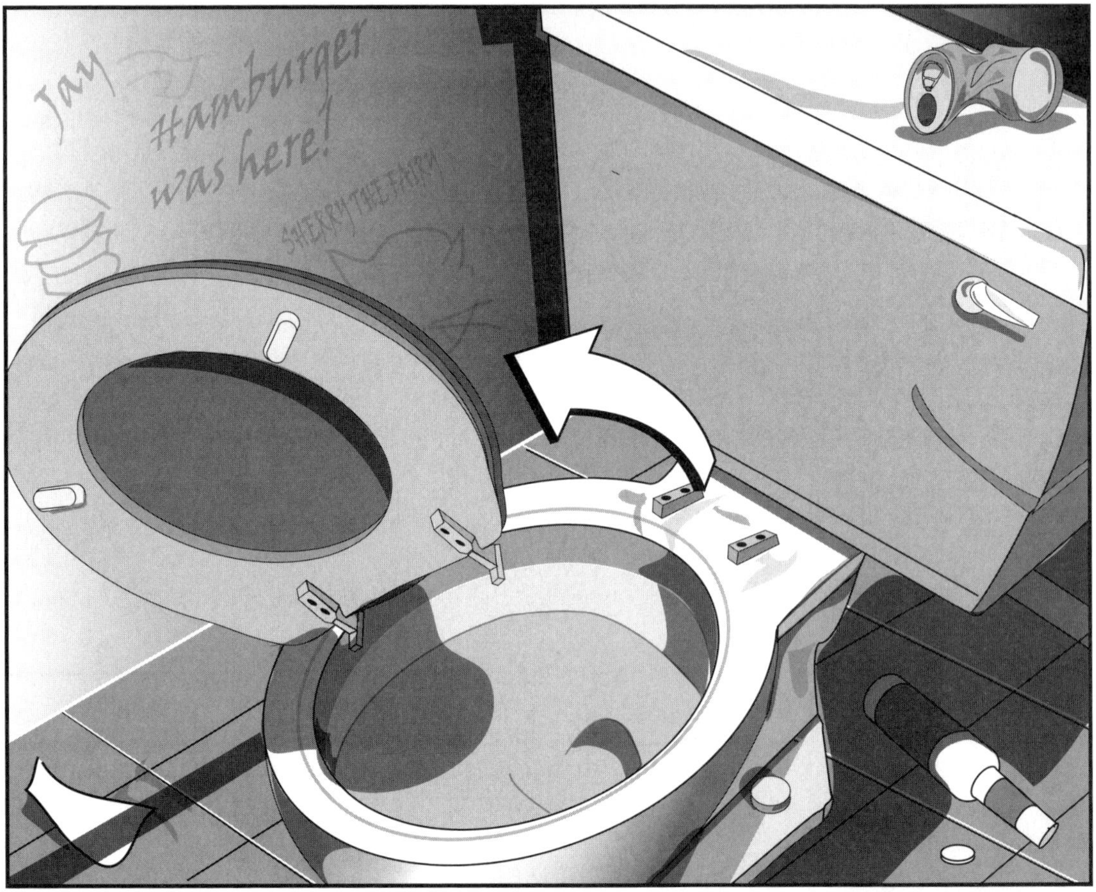

SUCCESSFUL ATTEMPTS

1	2	3	4	5	6	7	8	9	10	11	12	13	14	15	16	17

HAVE YOU EVER TRIED TO TAKE A DUMP WITHOUT TOUCHING THE SEAT? IT'S EXTREMELY DIFFICULT, AND VERY UNCOMFORTABLE. YOU FEEL LIKE A FRICKIN' FOOL ON A BOY SCOUT CAMPING TRIP, TRYING TO AVOID POISON IVY. NOW, YOU CAN INFLICT THIS HORROR ON YOUR ENEMIES. BEFORE YOU DO ANYTHING, GO BORROW YOUR ROOMMATE'S LATEX GLOVES, OR FIND A PAIR; YOU'LL NEED THEM. SNEAK INTO ANOTHER HALL'S BATHROOM, REMOVE ALL THE TOILET SEATS, AND TAKE THEM WITH YOU. YOU DON'T WANT TO GET CAUGHT, SO WHILE YOU UNSCREW THE HINGES, MAKE SURE THE STALL DOOR IS CLOSED. WHEN FINISHED, PROCEED TO THE NEXT STALL AND REPEAT THE STEP. WHAT YOU DO WITH THE SEATS IS YOUR CALL. PERHAPS SPELL OUT SOMETHING ON THE FOOTBALL FIELD?

ADDED BONUS: Using two-part epoxy, glue the seats in the upright position. The girls will try to lower them for twenty minutes before they give up!

PRANK UNIVERSITY

061 NUMBER THREE

SUCCESSFUL ATTEMPTS

1	2	3	4	5	6	7	8	9	10	11	12	13	14	15	16	17

THIS PRANK WORKS BEST ON PEOPLE YOU DON'T KNOW, SO GET YOUR CAMERA READY. THIS OPERATION WILL REQUIRE TWO FRIENDS AND A STRANGER. THE STRANGER IS THE POOR GUY WHO JUST HAD TO USE THE PORT-A-POTTY. YOUR FIRST FRIEND WILL PREPARE THE CAMERA, ABOUT TWENTY FEET IN FRONT OF THE DOOR. NOW, APPROACH THE PORT-A-POTTY WITH YOUR SECOND FRIEND AND BEGIN TALKING ABOUT HOW YOU SHOULD TIP IT OVER. START ROCKING THE PORTABLE RESTROOM. IF YOU'RE LUCKY, THE POOR GUY INSIDE WILL START YELLING, THEN QUICKLY RUN OUT BEFORE FINISHING HIS JOB. SEEING AS HIS PANTS WILL BE DOWN, HE'LL BE IN NO STATE TO RUN AFTER YOU. IF THERE IS A CONFRONTATION, JUST TELL HIM YOU THOUGHT YOUR FRIEND WAS IN THERE!

ADDED BONUS: If there are two port-a-potties and your friend is doing his duty in one of them, spin them toward each other so the doors won't open! This only works if there is no line.

PRANK UNIVERSITY

062 SUPERGLUE LIDS

SUCCESSFUL ATTEMPTS

1	2	3	4	5	6	7	8	9	10	11	12	13	14	15	16	17

SNEAK INTO THE FRIDGE ONE NIGHT AND SUPERGLUE VARIOUS JAR LIDS SHUT. IF THIS IS THE FIRST PRANK YOU PULL ON YOUR HOUSE-MATES, THEY WILL NEVER SUSPECT WHAT YOU'VE DONE. YOU WILL PROBABLY JUST REALLY UPSET YOUR ROOMMATES, SO I RECOMMEND PULLING THIS PRANK IN SOMEONE ELSE'S REFRIGERATOR. YOU CAN ALSO SUPERGLUE SOME OF THE BOTTLES TOGETHER, SO WHEN YOUR ROOMMATE NEEDS MAYO, HE GRABS THE MAYO, MUSTARD, AND SYRUP. THIS WORKS VERY WELL ON FOLKS WHO NEVER CLEAN OUT THE FRIDGE BECAUSE IT WILL BE FULL OF EMPTY, GLUED CONTAINERS.

ADDED BONUS: Switch your roommates' labels around. They will forget what kind of mustard they purchased.

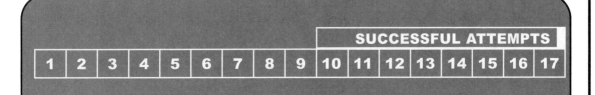

PRANK UNIVERSITY

063 UNSTABLE TABLE

140

SUCCESSFUL ATTEMPTS

1	2	3	4	5	6	7	8	9	10	11	12	13	14	15	16	17

HOLY UNSTABLE TABLE, COLLEGE FURNITURE SUCKS! UNLESS YOU'RE ONE OF A FEW PRIVILEGED KIDS, MOST OF THE FURNITURE IN YOUR ROOM IS PROBABLY EITHER HAND-ME-DOWNS FROM FRIENDS OF YOUR PARENTS OR FROM YOUR OLDER BROTHERS. YOU MAY EVEN HAVE A COLLECTION OF DUMPSTER-DIVING TREASURES! IF YOU PULL THIS PRANK OFF, DON'T FEEL BAD; YOUR FRIENDS WILL PROBABLY JUST FIX THE SHITTY FURNITURE WITH DUCT TAPE. YOU CAN EXECUTE THIS ON BEDS, TABLES, CHAIR LEGS, LOFT LADDERS, AND COUCHES BY SAWING INTO THE LEGS. THE TRICK TO A GOOD UNSTABLE TABLE IS TO NOT SAW *THROUGH* THE LEG; STOP SHORT, A LITTLE MORE THAN A QUARTER OF AN INCH. CLEAN UP ANY SAWDUST AND WALK AWAY LIKE NOTHING HAPPENED. YOUR ROOMMATE WILL KICK HIS FEET UP ON HIS TABLE, ONLY TO SEE IT CRUMBLE INTO PIECES.

ADDED BONUS: Keep the sawdust in a plastic cup. Weeks later, after you have pulled this prank, sprinkle some around his bed . . . mind games!

PRANK UNIVERSITY

064 IT'S A KEGGER

SUCCESSFUL ATTEMPTS

1	2	3	4	5	6	7	8	9	10	11	12	13	14	15	16	17

CONGRATULATIONS, IT'S A KEGGER! YOUR NEIGHBORS HAVE HAD A COUPLE OF HOUSE PARTIES, BUT NOTHING WORTH WRITING HOME ABOUT. TO HELP THOSE GUYS OUT, NEXT TIME THEY MAKE PLANS, YOU AND YOUR HOUSE OF FRIENDS DECIDE TO MAKE UP PARTY FLIERS AND DISTRIBUTE THEM LIKE MAD. PRINT HUNDREDS OF THEM, AND BEGIN POSTING THEM AROUND CAMPUS. OVERDO IT; PUT THEM EVERYWHERE! I SUGGEST RESTROOMS, ON TELEPHONE POLES, UNDER DORM DOORS—EVEN SEND THEM VIA INTER-CAMPUS MAIL. IF YOU ARE ESPECIALLY SPIRITED, YOU CAN WAIT OUTSIDE OF CLASSES TO HAND THEM OUT. YOUR NEIGHBORS WILL BE INNOCENTLY HAVING A PARTY WITH FORTY PEOPLE FRIDAY NIGHT WHEN MOBS OF THIRSTY PEOPLE BEGIN SHOWING UP! OF COURSE, DON'T LET THEM IN ON THE JOKE!

ADDED BONUS: Post party flyers around campus for a party at some stranger's house!

PRANK UNIVERSITY

065 DRUNK DRIVER

SUCCESSFUL ATTEMPTS

1	2	3	4	5	6	7	8	9	10	11	12	13	14	15	16	17

IT'S ALMOST IMPOSSIBLE TO GIVE AN EXACT MEASUREMENT FOR THE VOLUME OF THE MALE COLLEGE STUDENT'S BLADDER, BUT, EVENTUALLY, YOUR BUDDY IS GOING TO HAVE TO BREAK THE SEAL. HE MOTIONS TO YOU AS HE HEADS OFF TO THE ATM (AUTOMATED TINKLE MACHINE), AND YOU DECIDE TO JOIN HIM. YOU ACCOMPANY YOUR BUDDY INTO THE PUB'S RESTROOM AND PRETEND YOU ARE RELIEVING YOURSELF. AS HE BEGINS TO RID HIS BODY OF BEER PISS, SIMPLY GRAB HIS SHOULDER AND START SWINGING HIM FROM LEFT TO RIGHT. AS YOU'RE WHALING HIM ABOUT, YELL "DRUNK DRIVER!" SEVERAL TIMES. YOUR FRIEND WILL STRUGGLE TO KEEP HIS URINE ON TARGET!

ADDED BONUS: If your buddies insist on pulling this one on you, pretend to be doing the deed and, as they approach you, quickly turn around and fire!

PRANK UNIVERSITY

066 SALSA DREAMS

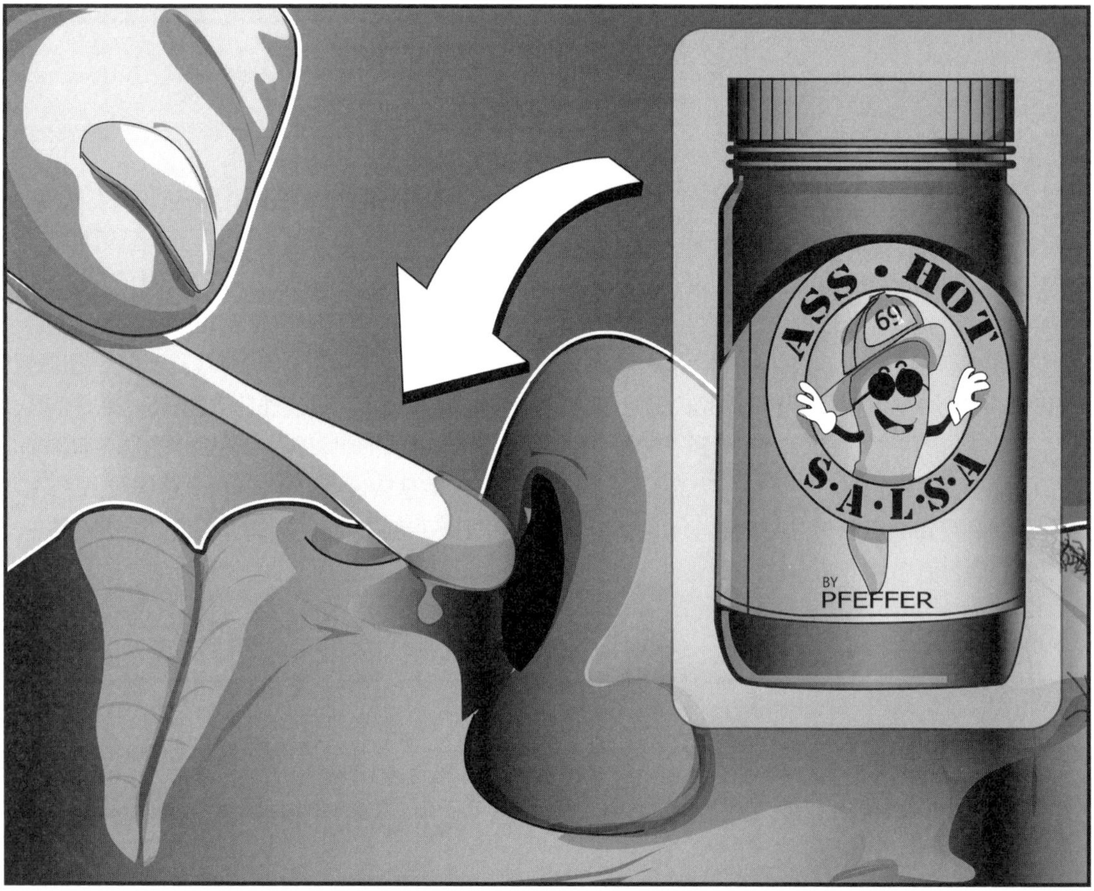

SUCCESSFUL ATTEMPTS																
1	2	3	4	5	6	7	8	9	10	11	12	13	14	15	16	17

SALSA—THAT SPICY MEXICAN SAUCE. YOU CAN USE SALSA FOR MANY THINGS, BUT DID YOU EVER THINK ABOUT PUTTING IT UP SOMEONE'S NOSE? LATE ONE NIGHT, WHEN YOUR FRIEND FALLS ASLEEP, GO GRAB SOME SALSA AND A Q-TIP. DON'T STICK THE Q-TIP IN THE SALSA; PLACE SALSA ON THE Q-TIP. NEXT, QUIETLY SLIDE THE Q-TIP UP YOUR BUDDY'S NOSE. HIS SENSES WILL GO WILD, AND HE WILL SURELY WAKE UP FARMER BLOWING. (FOR THOSE WHO MAY NOT KNOW WHAT A FARMER BLOW IS, IT'S A NOSE-CLEANING METHOD DONE WITHOUT USING PAPER PRODUCTS.) YOU FRIEND WILL HAVE THE MOST UNCOMFORTABLE FEELING FOR ABOUT AN HOUR AFTER THIS. IT'S HILARIOUS.

ADDED BONUS: Garlic on the lips will also produce a quick wake-up, and a run for the sink!

PRANK UNIVERSITY

067 DEAD MOUSE

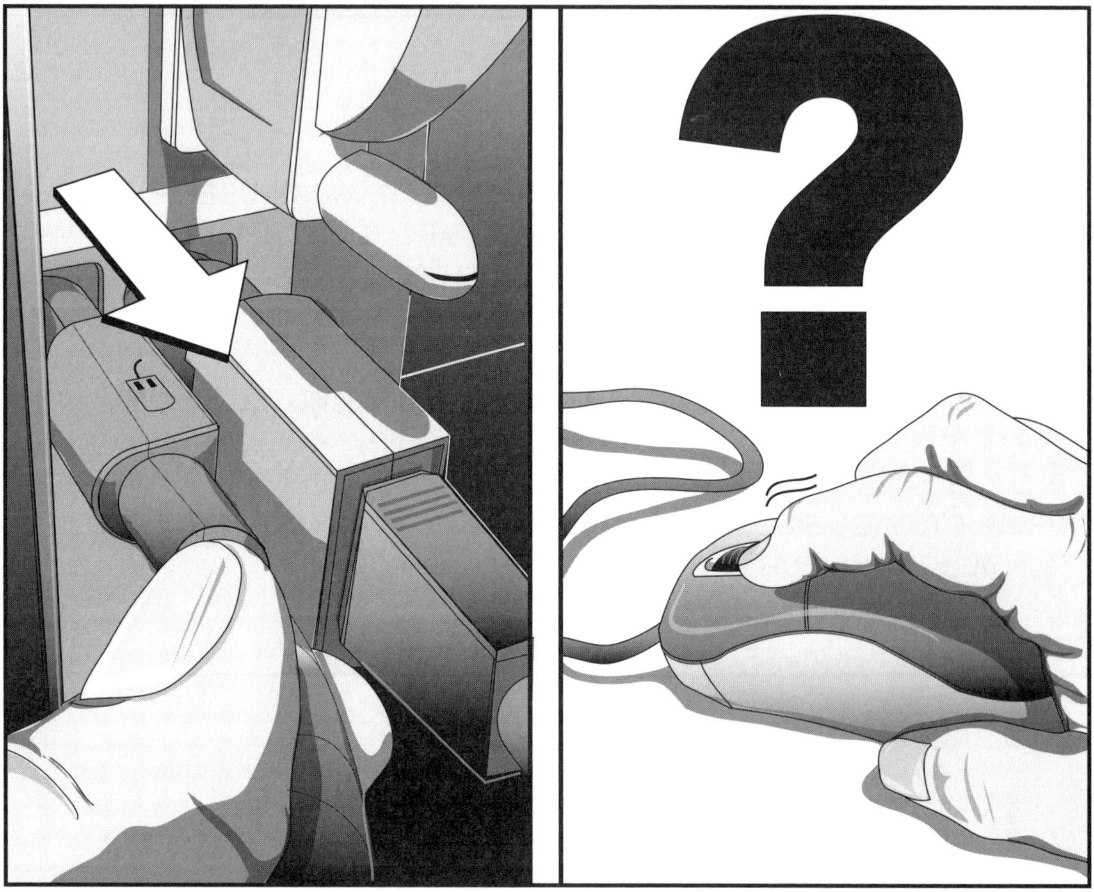

SUCCESSFUL ATTEMPTS

1	2	3	4	5	6	7	8	9	10	11	12	13	14	15	16	17

SOME STUDENTS ARE STILL COMPUTER ILLITERATE. IT'S A BAFFLING PHENOMENON THAT IN TODAY'S SOCIETY ANY STUDENT, WHO MIGHT IN OTHER CIRCUMSTANCES BE CONSIDERED SMART AND MODERN, WOULD SIT DOWN IN FRONT OF A COMPUTER SCREEN AND BECOME CLUELESS. SO, AS SIMPLE AS UNPLUGGING A COMPUTER MOUSE MAY SOUND, IT CAN STILL CONFUSE THESE ELECTRONIC VEGETABLES. THEY WILL RIGHT-CLICK FOR ABOUT A MINUTE BEFORE MOVING TO THE NEXT COMPUTER IN THE LAB. IT'S AMAZING HOW MANY PEOPLE REFUSE TO ASK FOR HELP IN THE COMPUTER LAB!

ADDED BONUS: Twist the bottom of the mouse and remove the ball. If it is an optical mouse, place a piece of tape or liquid paper over the light. Presto—dead mouse.

PRANK UNIVERSITY

068 SPIDERWEB

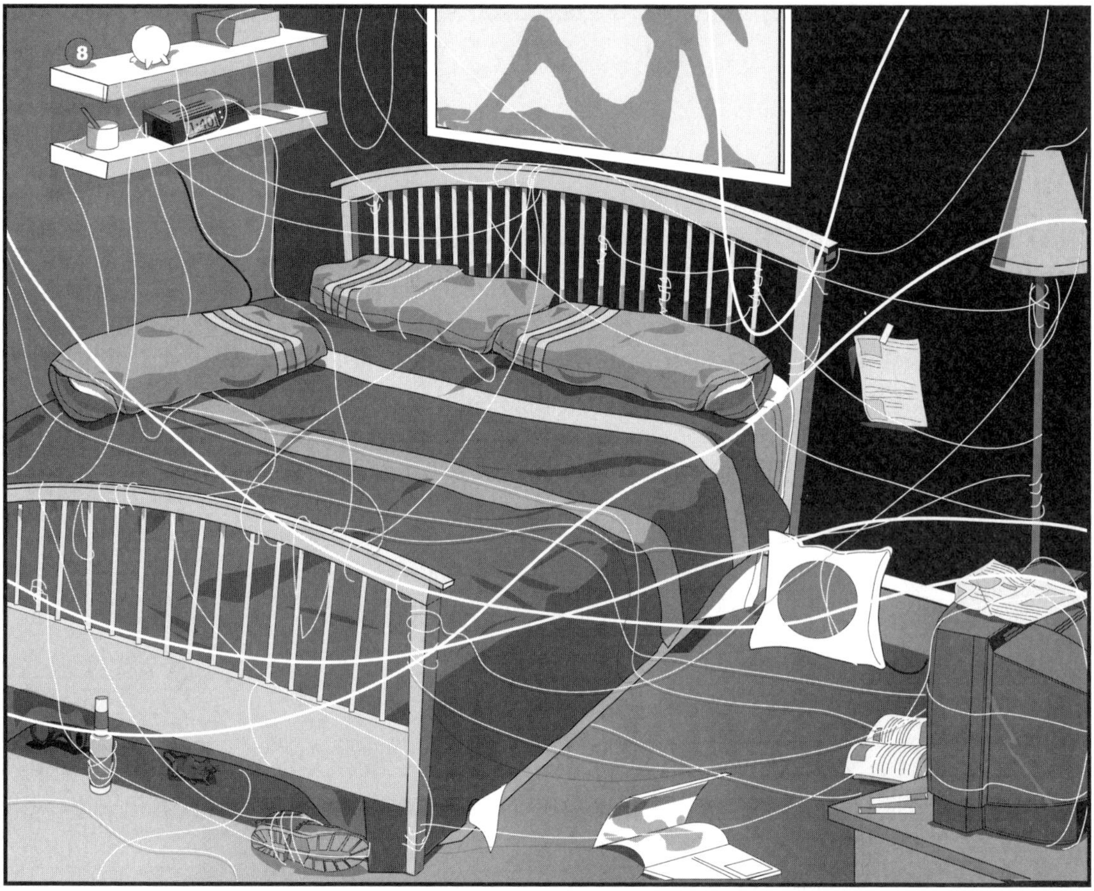

1 5 0

SUCCESSFUL ATTEMPTS

1	2	3	4	5	6	7	8	9	10	11	12	13	14	15	16	17

BEFORE YOU COMMIT TO THIS PRANK, YOU WILL NEED TO GO OUT AND BUY A COUPLE SPOOLS OF KITE STRING. ONCE YOU HAVE THE STRING, WE CAN BEGIN. STARTING AT THE BACK OF THE DORM ROOM, TIE EVERYTHING DOWN. CONTINUE TO TIE AS YOU MAKE YOUR WAY TO THE FRONT, WHERE THE DOOR IS LOCATED. I RECOMMEND YOU ALSO FILL A FEW MUGS WITH WATER AND TIE THE STRING TO THE HANDLES, SO WHEN YOUR ROOMMATE ENTERS THE ROOM, HE WILL START PULLING THE STRINGS OUT OF ANGER, AND MUGS WILL START TO DUMP.

ADDED BONUS: Use fishing line and tie everything six inches from the ground—then unscrew the lightbulb.

PRANK UNIVERSITY

069 PEEPHOLE REVERSE

SUCCESSFUL ATTEMPTS

1	2	3	4	5	6	7	8	9	10	11	12	13	14	15	16	17

THE PEEPHOLE IS AN AMAZING OPTICAL DEVICE. MOUNTED ON YOUR DORM-ROOM DOOR, IT ALLOWS YOU TO HAVE A CLEAR VIEW OF THE HALL OUTSIDE. WITH A SUPER-WIDE VIEWING ANGLE, IT LEAVES NO DEAD ZONE FOR INTRUDERS TO CONCEAL THEMSELVES. THE PEEPHOLE CAN BE REVERSED BY QUICKLY UNSCREWING IT FROM THE INSIDE. YOU WILL HAVE TO WAIT TILL YOUR COED NEIGHBOR GOES TO THE SHOWER, THEN QUICKLY UNSCREW IT AND REVERSE IT. THERE IS ONE CATCH—SHE'LL HAVE TO LEAVE THE DOOR UNLOCKED. THIS SAFEGUARD AGAINST UNEXPECTED VISITORS NOW BECOMES A FREE SHOW FOR UNEXPECTED VIEWERS!

ADDED BONUS: When in your room, you should always place a piece of tape over your peephole, so it looks like you're always looking out.

PRANK UNIVERSITY

070 LOCKED FOREVER

SUCCESSFUL ATTEMPTS																
1	2	3	4	5	6	7	8	9	10	11	12	13	14	15	16	17

LOCKERS MEET ALL YOUR SECURITY NEEDS, PROTECTING YOU FROM FIVE-FINGER DISCOUNTERS, BUT THEY CAN ALSO BE THE CAUSE OF MANY PROBLEMS: LOST KEYS, FORGOTTEN COMBINATIONS, OR THE UNTHINKABLE, A DOOR GLUED SHUT! A SMALL DROP OF EPOXY CAN QUICKLY SEAL ANY COMBINATION LOCK FOREVER. REMEMBER, BUILT-IN LOCKS ARE MAINTAINED AND OWNED BY THE INSTITUTE, SO ANY DAMAGE TO THOSE MAY RESULT IN A FINE OR PENALTY IF YOU ARE CAUGHT. I RECOMMEND HITTING UP PERSONAL PADLOCKS; IF YOU ARE CAUGHT, YOU WILL RECEIVE LESS HEAT.

ADDED BONUS: You can also rub the lock with an onion, so your victim's hands will stink every time he uses it!

PRANK UNIVERSITY

071 POLISH SEAT

SUCCESSFUL ATTEMPTS

1	2	3	4	5	6	7	8	9	10	11	12	13	14	15	16	17

FIRST, YOU HAVE TO FIND A SHOE POLISH THAT MATCHES THE COLOR OF THE TOILET SEAT. MAKE SURE YOU READ THE WARNING LABEL, TO MAKE SURE THE POLISH IS NOT HAZARDOUS. FINALLY, YOU MAY WANT TO WEAR GLOVES WHEN APPLYING THE POLISH; ANY POLISH ON YOUR HANDS COULD GIVE YOU AWAY. APPLY A GOOD AMOUNT OF SHOE POLISH TO THE SEAT; THE MORE YOU APPLY, THE LONGER IT WILL TAKE TO DRY. YOUR VICTIM WILL SIT ON THAT SEAT, AND WILL PROBABLY NOT NOTICE THE COLOR OF HIS BOTTOM TILL HE CHANGES CLOTHES LATER THAT DAY. THIS PRANK IS RATED LOW, AS MOST PEOPLE WIPE OFF A PUBLIC TOILET BEFORE SITTING DOWN—OR AT LEAST THEY SHOULD!

ADDED BONUS: Post signs around the dorm that brown spiders have been nesting under toilet seats and are extremely fatal. Word will spread like wildfire, and students will take a second look before sitting down.

PRANK UNIVERSITY

072 BALONEY SLICE

SUCCESSFUL ATTEMPTS

1	2	3	4	5	6	7	8	9	10	11	12	13	14	15	16	17

MY BALONEY HAS A FIRST NAME, AND IT'S A-U-T-O! THAT'S RIGHT, IN THIS PRANK YOU BALONEY-SLICE SOMEONE'S CAR. GO FIND THE CHEAPEST BALONEY YOU CAN, AND BUY A BUNCH OF IT. WHEN LAYING IT OUT, MAKE SURE YOU DISPERSE THE SLICES EVENLY. I SUGGEST DOING THIS AT NIGHT, WHEN THERE ARE USUALLY LESS PEOPLE AROUND TO SEE YOU. THE VICTIM OF THIS HEINOUS CRIME WILL FIND BALONEY ON THEIR HOOD, BOILING IN THE MORNING SUN! WHAT A SMELLY MESS TO CLEAN UP! BEWARE: I HAVE HEARD THAT CERTAIN PAINT/BALONEY COMBINATIONS WILL RESULT IN DAMAGE TO THE PAINT, WHICH COULD LEAD TO A FINE.

ADDED BONUS: You can also cover the car in baking powder or flour, and then add water!

PRANK UNIVERSITY

073 CLOUDY DAY

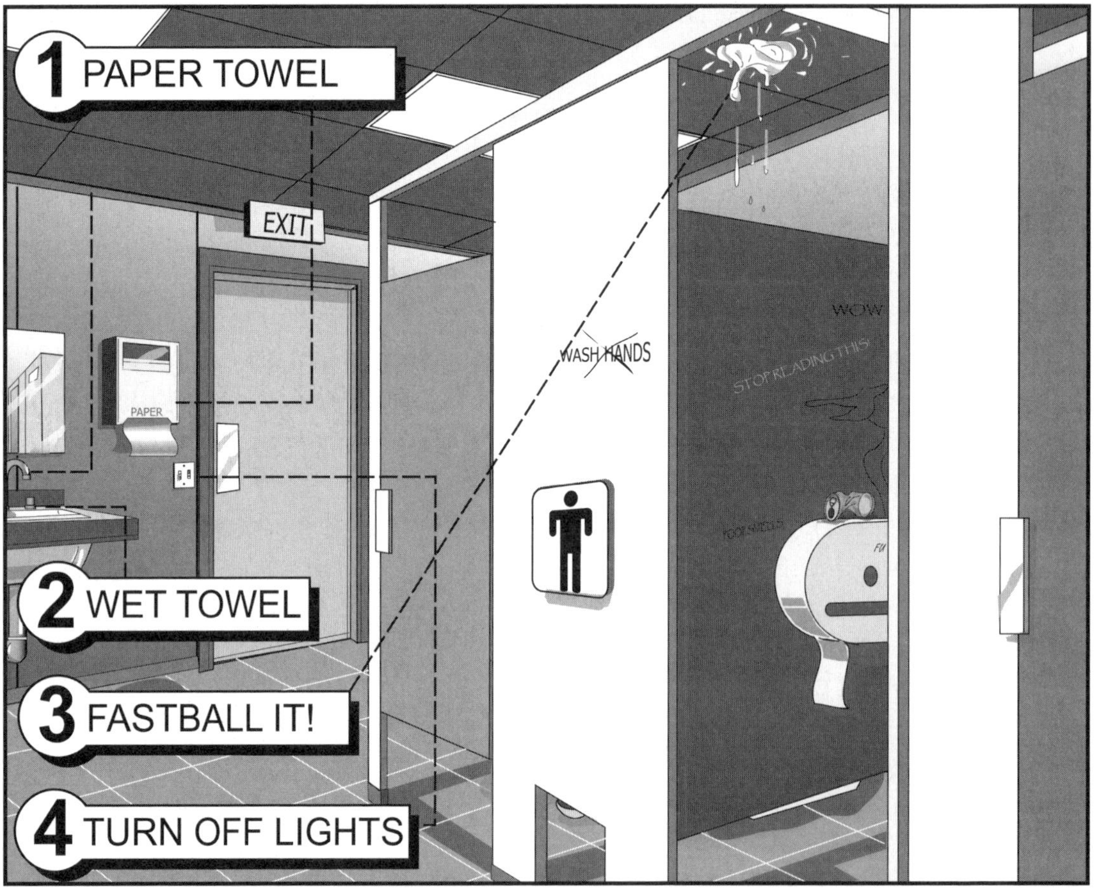

SUCCESSFUL ATTEMPTS

1	2	3	4	5	6	7	8	9	10	11	12	13	14	15	16	17

YOU'VE JUST WANDERED INTO THE BATHROOM AND NOTICE SOME FAMILIAR SNEAKERS IN ONE OF THE STALLS. YOU DECIDE TO PULL A LITTLE PRANK ON THIS GUY, SO YOU DON'T WANT TO LET HIM KNOW WHO YOU ARE. YOU WILL ALSO WANT TO STAY AWAY FROM THE CRACKS IN THE DOOR, AND MAKE SURE HE CAN'T SEE YOUR SHOES. IN FACT, YOU SHOULD WORK IN YOUR SOCKS. GO OVER TO THE PAPER TOWELS AND PULL OFF A COUPLE OF SHEETS. THEN, WET THE SHEETS IN THE SINK AND FORM A HUGE, WET BALL. THROW THE BALL RIGHT ABOVE YOUR VICTIM'S STALL; HOPEFULLY, IT WILL STICK TO THE CEILING. TURN OUT THE LIGHTS AND RUN. HE WILL BE SITTING ON THE TOILET, WONDERING WHERE AND WHAT THE HELL WHEN A LARGE BALL OF WET PAPER HEADS HIS WAY.

ADDED BONUS: Fill a plastic cup with water and toss it over the stall walls. It's a lame prank, but it will really piss the person off.

PRANK UNIVERSITY

074 MORNING OMELET

									SUCCESSFUL ATTEMPTS							
1	2	3	4	5	6	7	8	9	10	11	12	13	14	15	16	17

THIS IS VERY IMPORTANT: LATE ONE NIGHT, WHEN THE STOVE IS TURNED OFF AND HAS NOT BEEN IN USE FOR SOME TIME, POSITION A SINGLE FIRECRACKER UNDER ONE OF THE BURNERS. THE WICK SHOULD BE IN CONTACT WITH ONE OF THE HEATING ELEMENTS. THE FOLLOWING MORNING YOUR ROOMMATES WILL WAKE UP, AND THE MOTIVATED ONES WILL DECIDE TO MAKE SOMETHING ON THE STOVE. AFTER A FEW MINUTES, THE FIRECRACKER WILL EXPLODE AND, DEPENDING ON HOW YOUR KITCHEN IS SET UP, THIS COULD BE EARSPLITTING. A FIRECRACKER LEAVES VERY LITTLE EVIDENCE BEHIND, SO IT IS POSSIBLE THAT YOUR ROOMMATES WILL NOT FIGURE OUT THAT YOU HAD SOMETHING TO DO WITH THE STOVE BLOWOUT.

ADDED BONUS: Another great attention-getter is a small smoke bomb tucked under the burner.

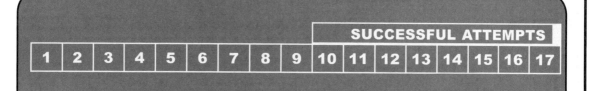

PRANK UNIVERSITY

075 FREEZING PEE

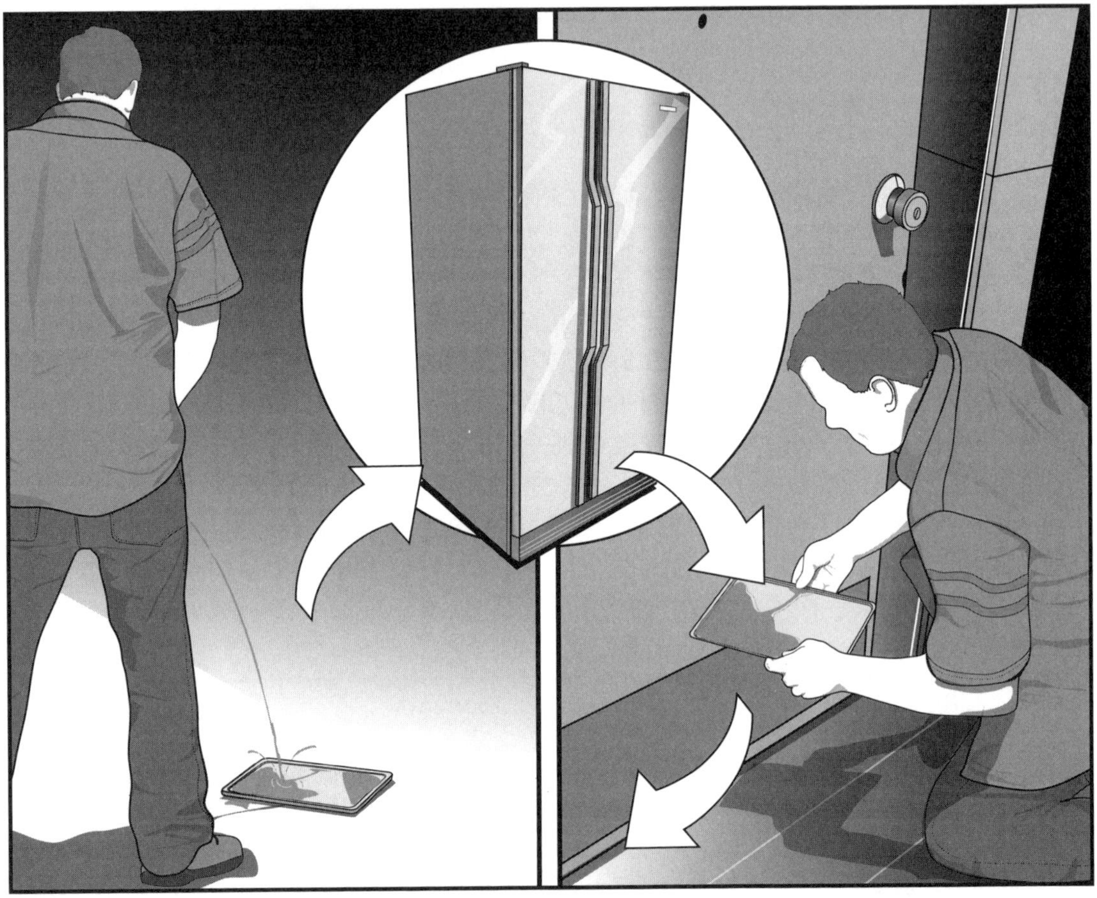

SUCCESSFUL ATTEMPTS

1	2	3	4	5	6	7	8	9	10	11	12	13	14	15	16	17

SOME PERSONALITIES IN DORM LAND DO NOT MESH WELL, DUE TO LACK OF HYGIENE, ALCOHOL ABUSE, OR SOMETHING CALLED STUDY TIME NOT BEING RESPECTED. SO, YOU PROBABLY HAVE SOME NEIGHBORS WHO HAVEN'T FOUND A COMMON BOND YET. LET'S ADD FUEL TO THAT FIRE. FIRST, YOU WILL NEED TO OBTAIN A STYROFOAM PANCAKE TRAY, WHICH CAN BE FOUND AT ANY FAST-FOOD JOINT. NEXT, URINATE ON THE TRAY, AND PLACE IT IN YOUR FREEZER. THEN SEPARATE THE FROZEN PEE FROM THE TRAY, AND SLIDE THE FROZEN PEE UNDER YOUR NEIGHBOR'S DOOR LATE ONE NIGHT. DURING THE NIGHT THE PEE WILL MELT, AND BY MORNING IT WILL APPEAR THAT ONE OF THE ROOMMATES HAS DECIDED TO URINATE ON THE FLOOR AFTER A WILD NIGHT OF DRINKING. THE QUESTION IS, WHICH ONE?

ADDED BONUS: Straighten a wire hanger, and use it to push the tray five or six feet into the room. Prank them several times in one month!

PRANK UNIVERSITY

076 ITCHY UNDIES

COLLEGE
FLASHCARDS

TIGHTY-WHITIES

ITCHING POWDER

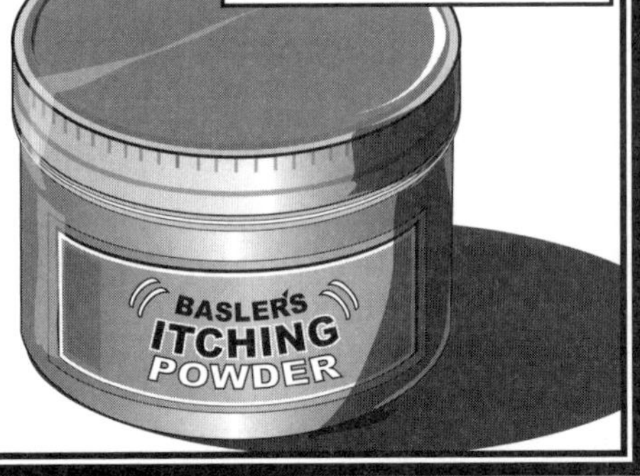

SUCCESSFUL ATTEMPTS																
1	2	3	4	5	6	7	8	9	10	11	12	13	14	15	16	17

COLLEGE MATH 101: TIGHTY-WHITIES PLUS ITCHING POWDER EQUALS ONE UNHAPPY YOUNG MAN. THIS PRANK IS REALLY SIMPLE. THE FIRST STEP IS TO LOCATE A CONTAINER OF THIS MYSTERIOUS ITCHING POWDER ON THE INTERNET. NEXT, GO INTO YOUR ROOMMATE'S DRESSER AND SPRINKLE SOME POWDER IN HIS UNDERPANTS. HE WILL THINK HE HAS DEVELOPED SOME KIND OF CROTCH ROT AND WILL PROBABLY GO OUT AND BUY ANTIFUNGAL SPRAY TO RELIEVE THE ITCHING AND BURNING. BEWARE: I RECOMMEND *NOT* GETTING CAUGHT IN YOUR ROOMMATE'S UNDERWEAR DRAWER—THAT SITUATION WILL MAKE BOTH OF YOU FEEL VERY UNCOMFORTABLE. THIS PRANK HAS BEEN PROVEN CLINICALLY EFFECTIVE IN THE TREATMENT OF ANY MEATHEAD WITH ATTITUDE.

ADDED BONUS: As your roommate is sleeping, sprinkle itching powder down his back, and film him itching and rolling around.

PRANK UNIVERSITY

077 DOORBELL DITCH

SUCCESSFUL ATTEMPTS

1	2	3	4	5	6	7	8	9	10	11	12	13	14	15	16	17

KNOWN AS BOTH "DING-DONG DITCH" AND "DOORBELL DITCH," THIS CHILDHOOD GAME NEVER GETS OLD. IT'S THE GAME WHERE YOU RING A PERSON'S DOORBELL OR KNOCK ON THEIR DORM DOOR AND THEN RUN AWAY TO HIDE IN A NEARBY BUSH OR HALLWAY. DO NOT LET THE PRANKEE SEE YOU, BECAUSE THAT IS THE PUNCH LINE OF THE DOORBELL DITCH. TEAM UP WITH A FRIEND, AND HAVE HIM HANDLE THE VIDEO CAMERA! I RECOMMEND HITTING UP THE SAME HOUSE A COUPLE OF TIMES, BUT DON'T HANG AROUND TOO LONG, JUST IN CASE A SQUAD CAR IS CALLED INTO HOT PURSUIT. ALSO, PICK YOUR NEIGHBORHOOD WISELY; SOME PEOPLE ARE DISGRUNTLED AND OWN GUNS!

ADDED BONUS: Combine with Prank #1, "Bag of Poo," for a winning combination and a great movie!

PRANK UNIVERSITY

078 DVD SWITCH

SUCCESSFUL ATTEMPTS

1	2	3	4	5	6	7	8	9	10	11	12	13	14	15	16	17

FOR SOME REASON YOUR ROOMMATE IS THE KING OF DVD LAND. WITH HUNDREDS OF NEW AND CLASSIC TITLES, HE'S IDOLIZED BY ALL THE OTHER BASEMENT-DWELLERS ON YOUR FLOOR. EVERY DAY, THEY TALK ABOUT SPECIAL EDITIONS, DELETED SCENES, AND THAT GUY EXPOSING HIMSELF IN THE CROWD AT THE END OF *TEEN WOLF.* EVEN SCARIER THAN *FRIDAY THE 13TH,* HE'S GOT THEM IN ALPHABETICAL ORDER, AND HE GETS ROYALLY PISSED WHEN YOU PLACE *GOODFELLAS* BEHIND *RAMBO.* WELL, IF THAT PISSES HIM OFF, THIS IS GOING TO MAKE HIM CRAP HIS PANTS! RANDOMLY SWITCH ALL THE DISCS IN THE CASES. EVEN THROW A FEW MUSIC CDS IN SOME OF THEM. WHEN SHERLOCK HOLMES FIGURES OUT WHAT HAS HAPPENED TO HIS COLLECTION IT COULD BECOME DANGEROUS, SO BE SURE TO BLAME IT ON SOMEONE ELSE.

ADDED BONUS: Every guy has a few "chick" movies that he breaks out when the old lady is over. Place a few quality adult movies in those cases. She'll be very surprised when she sees *Cheerleader Club XI* in the *Sleepless in Seattle* case.

PRANK UNIVERSITY

079 PINK WHITIES

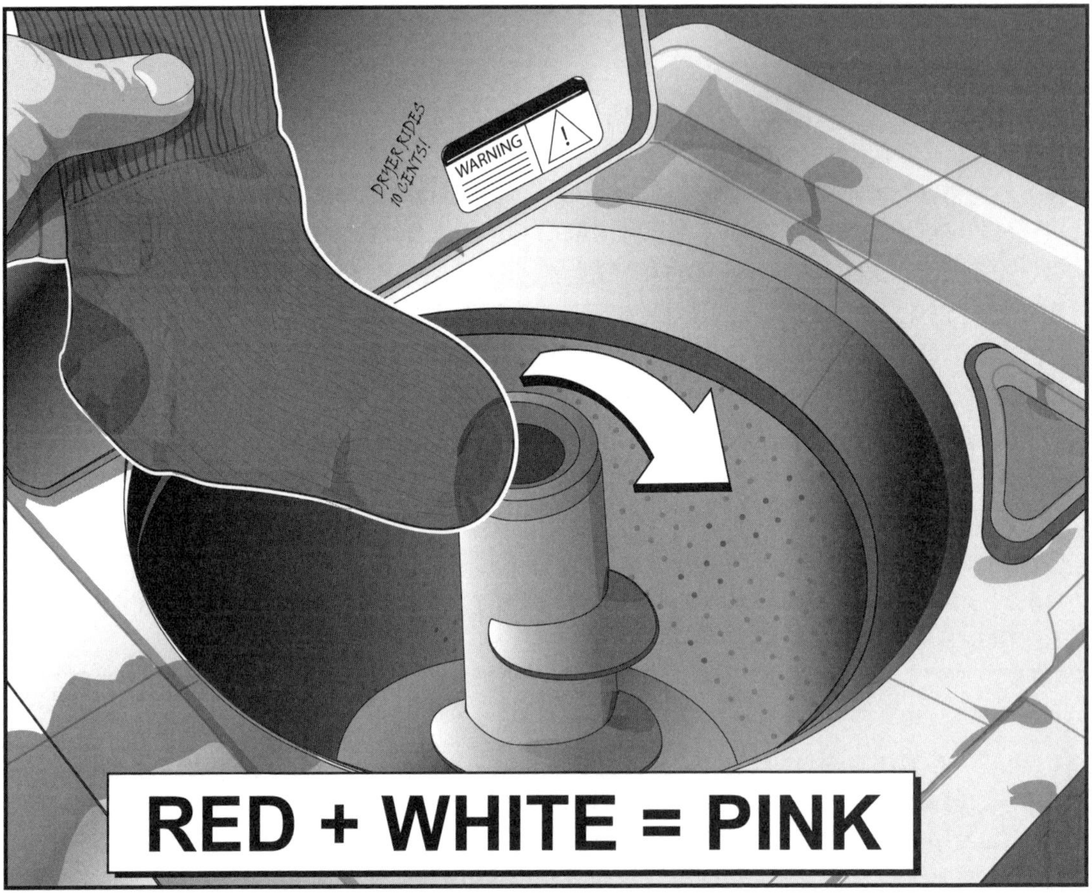

3

SUCCESSFUL ATTEMPTS

1	2	3	4	5	6	7	8	9	10	11	12	13	14	15	16	17

TAKE A STROLL DOWN TO THE LAUNDRY ROOM AND ADD BRIGHT RED SOCKS TO PEOPLE'S WHITIES LOADS. IN ORDER TO FIND OUT BEFOREHAND IF THE SOCK WILL ACTUALLY BLEED COLOR, PUT A DROP OF WATER ON IT, AND THEN BLOT IT WITH A WHITE TOWEL OR A COTTON BALL. IF THE COLOR COMES OFF, YOU HAVE A WINNER. IF YOUR LAUNDRY HAS TURNED PINK BECAUSE SOMEONE EVIL HAS ADDED A GARMENT OF THE WRONG COLOR, FOLLOW THIS HINT: FIRST, REMOVE THE OFFENDING ARTICLE, THEN IMMEDIATELY RUN THE WASHING MACHINE THROUGH ANOTHER COMPLETE CYCLE. YOU CAN ALSO ADD A "COLOR REMOVER," WHICH WORKS WONDERS FOR RETURNING ITEMS BACK TO BRIGHT WHITE.

ADDED BONUS: Add a ton of soap to the washing machines when no one's looking. It will bring back memories of foam parties during spring break.

PRANK UNIVERSITY

080 ILLEGAL DOWNLOADS

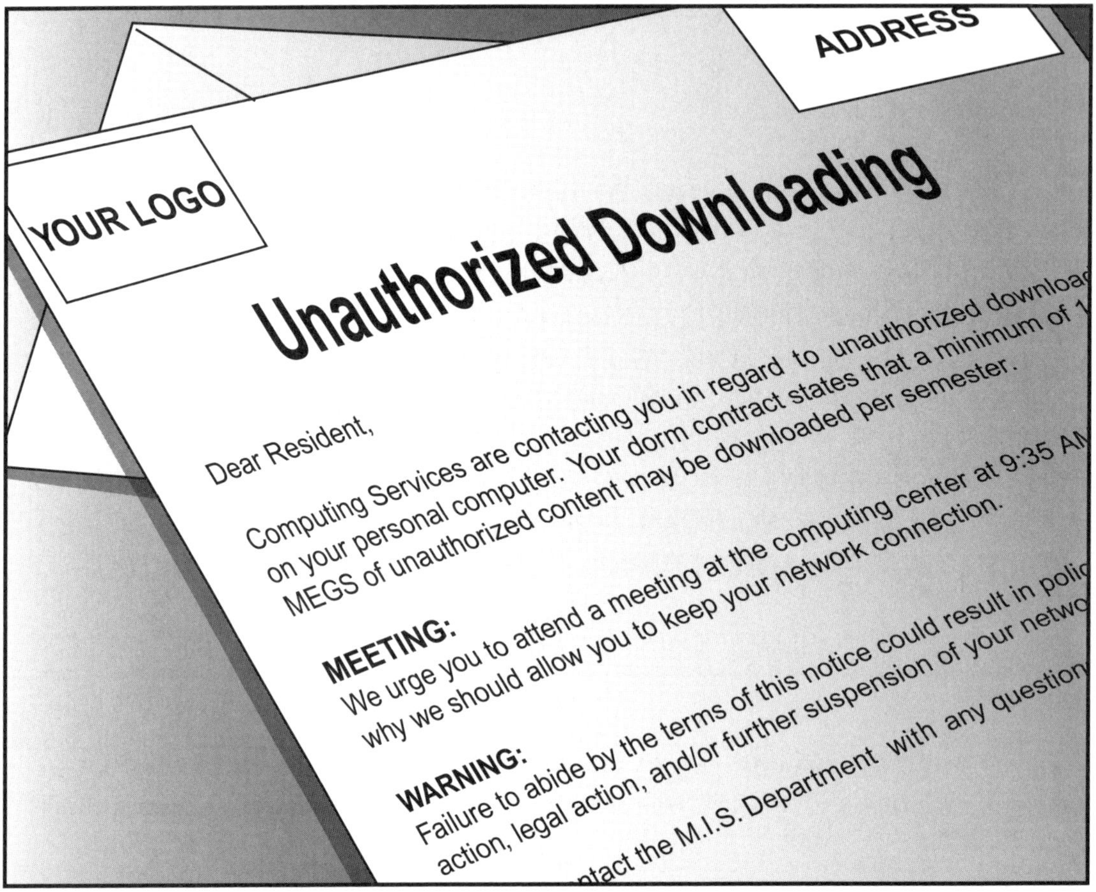

ADDRESS
YOUR LOGO
Unauthorized Downloading
Dear Resident,
Computing Services are contacting you in regard to unauthorized downloa
on your personal computer. Your dorm contract states that a minimum of 1
MEGS of unauthorized content may be downloaded per semester.
MEETING:
We urge you to attend a meeting at the computing center at 9:35 A
why we should allow you to keep your network connection.
WARNING:
Failure to abide by the terms of this notice could result in polic
action, legal action, and/or further suspension of your netwo
ntact the M.I.S. Department with any question

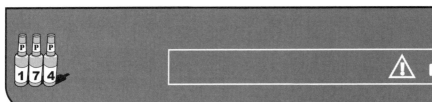

SUCCESSFUL ATTEMPTS

1	2	3	4	5	6	7	8	9	10	11	12	13	14	15	16	17

DOWNLOADING AND FILE-SHARING ON THE INTERNET HAVE RECEIVED A LOT OF ATTENTION FROM LEGISLATORS OVER THE LAST FEW YEARS. YOUR ROOMMATE OR NEIGHBOR HAS PROBABLY BEEN TINKERING WITH THIS ILLEGAL ACTIVITY DURING THE COURSE OF THE YEAR. EVERYONE HAS HEARD OF THE HUGE LAWSUITS INSTIGATED BY THE MUSIC INDUSTRY AND THE MOTION PICTURE ASSOCIATION TO CRACK DOWN ON INTERNET DOWNLOADERS. TO SCARE THE HELL OUT OF YOUR DOWNLOAD-HAPPY NEIGHBOR, WRITE UP A FAKE LETTER FROM A FAKE LAW FIRM, INCLUDING HIS USERNAME IF POSSIBLE, STATING KNOWLEDGE OF THIS ACT ON HIS PERSONAL COMPUTER. MENTION SUSPENSION AND A POSSIBLE FINE IF HE DOES NOT CONTACT THE CAMPUS COMPUTER-SERVICES DEPARTMENT. MAKE SURE YOU USE A PRINTED ENVELOPE WITH A PREPAID POSTMARK.

ADDED BONUS: You could also send the same letter home to his parents. You can always include his "favorite" sites, which he loves to visit when no one is home.

PRANK UNIVERSITY

081 FISH FRY

SUCCESSFUL ATTEMPTS

1	2	3	4	5	6	7	8	9	10	11	12	13	14	15	16	17

HONEY, WHAT IS THAT SMELL?" YOU'D NEVER IMAGINE THAT SOMEONE PUT A DEAD FISH UNDER YOUR HOOD. TO PULL OFF THIS MISCHIEVOUS ACT YOU WILL NEED TO ACQUIRE YOUR VICTIM'S CAR KEYS. YOU CAN SIMPLY STEAL THEM, OR NICELY ASK TO BORROW THE CAR. IF HE SAYS YES, YOU'RE IN. NOW, DRIVE HIS CAR TO THE NEAREST GROCERY STORE OR SHORELINE, AND TRY TO LOCATE A GOOD-SIZED DEAD FISH, ONE WORTHY OF THIS CAR. WHEN YOU ARE WITHIN A BLOCK OF HIS HOUSE, PULL OVER AND PLACE THE FISH UNDER THE HOOD. IT WILL PROBABLY TAKE YOUR VICTIM A FEW DAYS TO LOOK UNDER THE HOOD. THIS PRANK WORKS BEST RIGHT BEFORE HE GOES ON A LONG TRIP OR DRIVES HOME FOR A HOLIDAY BREAK.

ADDED BONUS: A fish can be pretty nasty, but roadkill is just mean! People might think you are twisted for taking a squirrel off the road, but you're okay with that, right?

PRANK UNIVERSITY

082 SLOPPY KNOB

									SUCCESSFUL ATTEMPTS							
1	2	3	4	5	6	7	8	9	10	11	12	13	14	15	16	17

ARE YOUR DORM NEIGHBORS THE TYPE WHO INSIST ON LEAVING THEIR DOOR OPEN WHEN THEY SMOKE, PARTY, OR WATCH A MOVIE IN SURROUND SOUND? IF YOU FIND THIS EXTREMELY RUDE, GET THEM BACK. YOUR NEIGHBOR JUST RAN TO THE SHOWER. QUICKLY RUN OUT AND PUT PETROLEUM JELLY ON HIS DOORKNOB. WHEN HE RETURNS HE WILL HAVE A VERY DIFFICULT TIME TURNING THE KNOB. THIS PRANK ALSO WORKS WELL FOR CLASSROOM DOORS AND DRAWER KNOBS. IT'S FAIRLY SIMPLE, AND THE RATING REFLECTS THAT, BUT IT IS EFFECTIVE AND WILL FRUSTRATE PEOPLE, AND THAT'S THE POINT OF THIS BOOK.

ADDED BONUS: Have some extra petroleum jelly? Place a bunch in your palm and casually walk up to your neighbor for a good, firm handshake, then run like hell.

PRANK UNIVERSITY

083 MISSING EYEBROWS

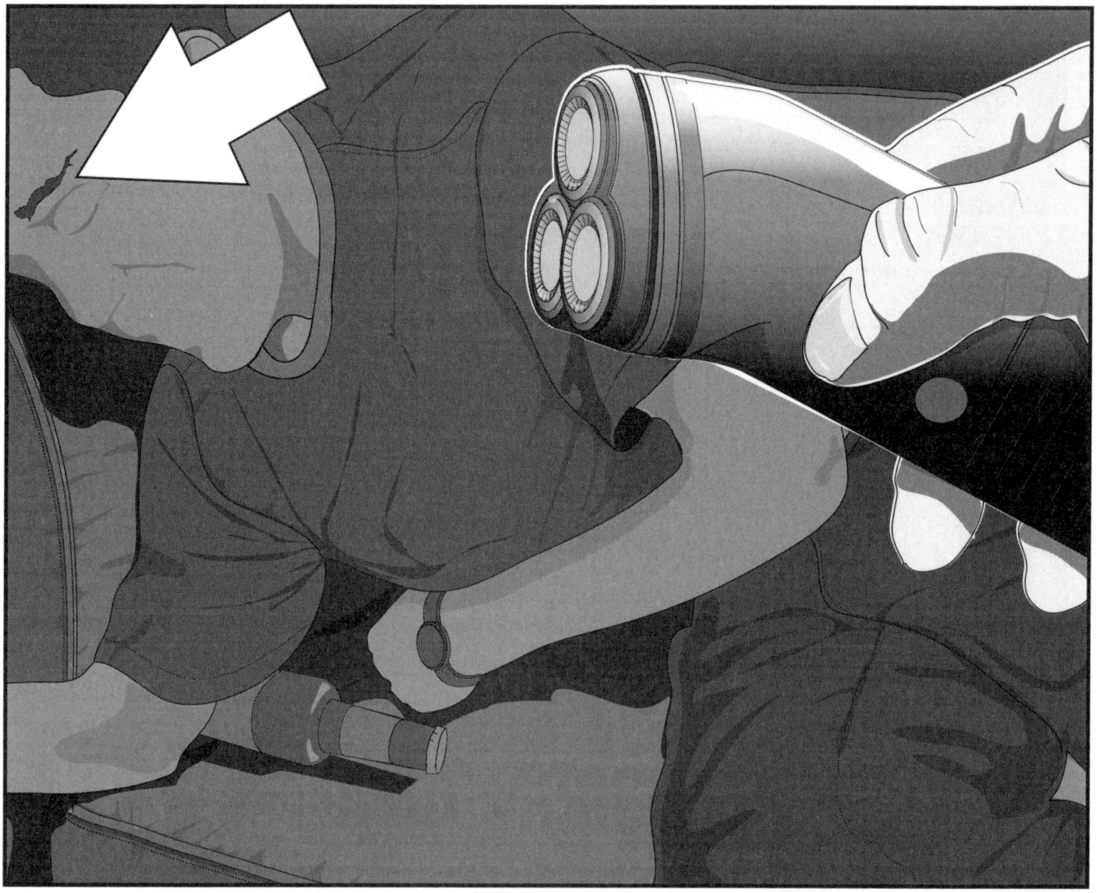

SUCCESSFUL ATTEMPTS

1	2	3	4	5	6	7	8	9	10	11	12	13	14	15	16	17

THE VICTIM OF YOUR VENGEANCE IS SNORING SO SOUNDLY, WASTED ON BEER AND CHEAP COCKTAILS. IT IS ONLY CUSTOMARY TO PLAY A PRANK ON THIS UNCONSCIOUS STUDENT—PAYBACK FOR HIS PREVIOUS PRANKS ON YOU. YOU QUICKLY GRAB THE RAZOR AND START IN ON HIS THICK EYEBROWS. YOU WILL WANT TO APPLY THE RAZOR SOFTLY SO YOU DO NOT WAKE HIM. EVENTUALLY HE WILL WAKE UP ON HIS OWN AND SEE HIS REFLECTION AND HIS ABSURD APPEARANCE. THE VICTIM WILL SURELY SEEK REVENGE. MY ADVICE TO YOU IS THIS: DON'T BE THE FIRST TO FALL ASLEEP FOR A WHILE, AND HIDE THIS BOOK.

ADDED BONUS: Don't stop there. Shave a widow's peak into his head, and help him start the balding process. He will have to go to class like that for weeks!

PRANK UNIVERSITY

084 LOTION MOTION

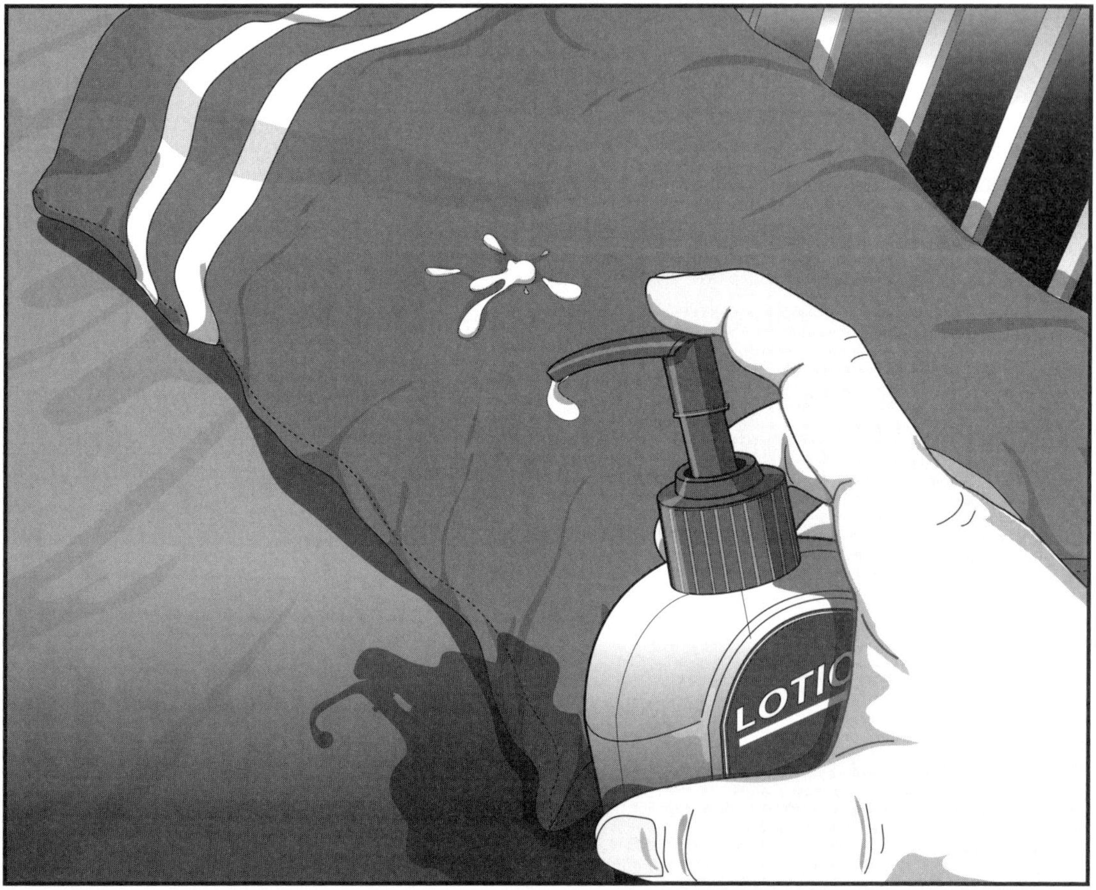

SUCCESSFUL ATTEMPTS

1	2	3	4	5	6	7	8	9	10	11	12	13	14	15	16	17

YOUR ROOMMATE IS OUT POURING DRAFT, AND YOU ARE LEFT AT HOME ALONE, DOING HOMEWORK IN YOUR ROOM. THERE COMES A POINT IN MANY ROOMMATE RELATIONSHIPS WHERE WE FIND OURSELVES DRIFTING AWAY FROM EACH OTHER. HE'S GOT HIS FRIENDS, AND YOU'VE GOT YOUR HOMEWORK. HE MIGHT BE OUT HAVING A BLAST, BUT YOU HAVE ALL HIS STUFF TO MESS WITH WHEN HE'S GONE! TAKE A LITTLE LOTION AND SQUIRT SOME ON HIS PILLOWCASE—BUT LESS IS MORE HERE. THIS PRANK WORKS GREAT IN A HOUSE FULL OF GUYS. THE MORE SUSPECTS, THE LESS LIKELY YOU ARE TO BE FOUND GUILTY.

ADDED BONUS: Combine this with Prank #50, "Sleepover," for the "icing on the cake."

PRANK UNIVERSITY

085 WHAT'S THAT NOISE?

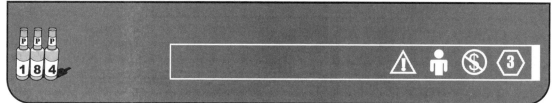

SUCCESSFUL ATTEMPTS

1	2	3	4	5	6	7	8	9	10	11	12	13	14	15	16	17

SOME PEOPLE GRADUATE FROM HIGH SCHOOL, BUT DON'T GRADUATE FROM THEIR HIGH-SCHOOL CARS. OUR CARS WERE OUR FREEDOM BACK IN HIGH SCHOOL, BUT IN COLLEGE THEY HAVE BECOME OUR NIGHTMARE. YOU ARE CONSTANTLY VISITING THE MECHANIC, CALLING DAD, AND—WORST OF ALL—PAYING PARKING VIOLATIONS! IF YOU WANT TO MESS WITH YOUR FRIEND'S RIDE, CRAWL UNDERNEATH AND TIE A BUNCH OF CANS TO THE FRAMEWORK. MAKE SURE THEY TOUCH THE PAVEMENT, SO THEY ONLY MAKE NOISE WHEN HE HITS A BUMP OR ACCELERATES.

ADDED BONUS: Round up your pals and hit up the entire student parking lot. Try to add cans to as many cars as possible.

PRANK UNIVERSITY

086 TIME TO CATCH UP

SUCCESSFUL ATTEMPTS																
1	2	3	4	5	6	7	8	9	10	11	12	13	14	15	16	17

WAKING UP FOR AN EARLY CLASS IS ALREADY A HEADACHE. THE ONLY THING WORSE IS TAKING A SHOWER ONLY TO FIND THAT SOME JACK-ASS HAS PUT KETCHUP IN YOUR SHAMPOO! THIS WORKS GREAT IN THE DORMS, BUT EVEN BETTER AT HOUSE PARTIES, SINCE THEY ARE ALWAYS PRETTY NUTS. ONCE IN A WHILE THE HOSTS MIGHT LET YOU USE THE "GOOD" BATHROOM UPSTAIRS—A PERFECT OPPORTUNITY TO STRIKE. DEFINITELY DO IT IF YOU HATE THE GUYS! THIS ALSO WORKS GREAT AT THE GYM.

ADDED BONUS: At most parties, you'll be walking around with a beer. Throw some of that in the shampoo, too, but not too much. It's beer, for God's sake!

PRANK UNIVERSITY

087 AVALANCHE

5

SUCCESSFUL ATTEMPTS

1	2	3	4	5	6	7	8	9	10	11	12	13	14	15	16	17

IT'S THE LAST EVENING BEFORE FINAL EXAMS, AND EVERYONE IS BUSY CRAMMING FOR TOMORROW'S TESTS. YOUR POOR, FRETFUL NEIGHBOR HAS BEEN IN HIS ROOM ALL NIGHT LONG AND REFUSES TO BE DISTURBED BY VISITORS. THUS, HE HAS GIVEN YOU THE PERFECT OPPORTUNITY TO PULL OFF THE "AVALANCHE." TAKE A TRIP TO THE LOCAL CLUB STORE AND BUY TWO OR THREE OF THOSE HUGE BAGS OF FAKE YELLOW POPCORN THAT TASTES LIKE CRAP. IN YOUR ROOM, START PREPARING THE PIECES OF TAPE—THAT WAY, THE VICTIM CAN'T HEAR ANY NOISE OUTSIDE HIS DOOR. TAPE A CLOSED TRASH BAG IN FRONT OF HIS DOOR, ON THE DOORJAMB, AND THEN FILL THE POUCH WITH POPCORN. THE TRASH BAG IS ONLY SERVING AS THE FOURTH WALL; CARDBOARD CAN BE SUBSTITUTED. IF YOU WANT, YOU CAN GO ALL THE WAY UP TO THE TOP. KNOCK ON HIS DOOR AND RUN LIKE HELL.

ADDED BONUS: Packing peanuts also work great and are impossible to vacuum up!

PRANK UNIVERSITY

088 SURPRISE PARTY

									SUCCESSFUL ATTEMPTS							
1	2	3	4	5	6	7	8	9	10	11	12	13	14	15	16	17

WELL, IT'S THAT TIME OF THE YEAR: FRESHMAN MOVING DAY. THEY ARE STARTING A NEW LIFE, ALL OF THEIR HIGH-SCHOOL STEREOTYPES HAVE BEEN DISMISSED, AND NOW THEY HAVE A CLEAN SLATE. WHY NOT MAKE THEM FEEL WELCOME BY THROWING THEM A PARTY? BUT THIS PARTY IS GOING TO BE A LITTLE DIFFERENT. THE INVITE LIST HAS ONLY BALLOONS ON IT—HUNDREDS OF THEM. FILL A NEW FRESHMAN'S ROOM WITH AS MANY BALLOONS AS YOU AND YOUR ACCOMPLICES CAN BLOW UP. YOU WILL NEED ACCESS TO HER ROOM WHILE SHE IS OUT, BUT BEING AN UPPERCLASSMAN, THAT SHOULDN'T BE TOO HARD FOR YOU.

ADDED BONUS: Mix a few water balloons in with the batch, just in case they come in with knives blazing!

PRANK UNIVERSITY

089 ALARM WITH REPORT

SUCCESSFUL ATTEMPTS

1	2	3	4	5	6	7	8	9	10	11	12	13	14	15	16	17

ANY RESPECTABLE COLLEGE DWELLING HAS A PERSONAL HOARD OF FIREWORKS; IT WOULD BE A CRIME NOT TO. NOW YOU CAN PUT THEM TO GOOD USE. YOUR ROOMMATE HAS DECIDED TO GO FOR THE NEW GUINNESS SLEEPING RECORD; HE'S BEEN IN BED FOR ALMOST ELEVEN HOURS! ABSORBED IN HIS BUZZING DREAMS, HE QUIETLY CONTINUES WITH HIS NATURAL SUSPENSION OF CONSCIOUSNESS. YOU SECRETLY ENTER THE ROOM WITH A HANDFUL OF "ENCOURAGEMENT" FOR THE SLEEPING BEAUTY. YOU LIGHT A CELEBRATION WORTHY OF INDEPENDENCE DAY AND RUN. MOST LIKELY, YOUR ROOMMATE HAS JUST SOILED HIMSELF. BUT, BEWARE: FIREWORKS IN THE DORM COULD LEAD TO SUSPENSION OR REMOVAL.

ADDED BONUS: Combine with Prank #45, "Lights Out in Chinatown," for extra fun.

PRANK UNIVERSITY

090 HAIRY DEODORANT

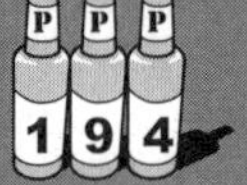

SUCCESSFUL ATTEMPTS

1	2	3	4	5	6	7	8	9	10	11	12	13	14	15	16	17

THERE IS NO SUCH THING AS PROPER BATHROOM ETIQUETTE IN COLLEGE. IT JUST DOESN'T EXIST. YOU WILL BE LUCKY IF YOUR ROOMMATE BUYS TOILET PAPER WHEN YOU RUN OUT! THAT SAID, IT IS YOUR DIVINE RIGHT TO MAKE YOUR ROOMMATE'S LIFE AS MISERABLE AS POSSIBLE. PLACE A SMALL QUANTITY OF YOUR OWN CURLY BODY HAIR ON YOUR ROOMMATE'S DEODORANT STICK. HE WILL PROBABLY NOT NOTICE THE FOREIGN HAIRS AT FIRST, BUT EVENTUALLY HE'LL SPOT THEM. PULL THIS PRANK OFF SEVERAL TIMES DURING THE WEEK. DON'T FESS UP TO THE CRIME; INSTEAD, FRAME SOMEONE ELSE IN THE HOUSE!

ADDED BONUS: Shave off all the deodorant and rub down the ends so it appears that someone has used it all up. Do this several times a year!

PRANK UNIVERSITY

091 BIKE LOCKDOWN

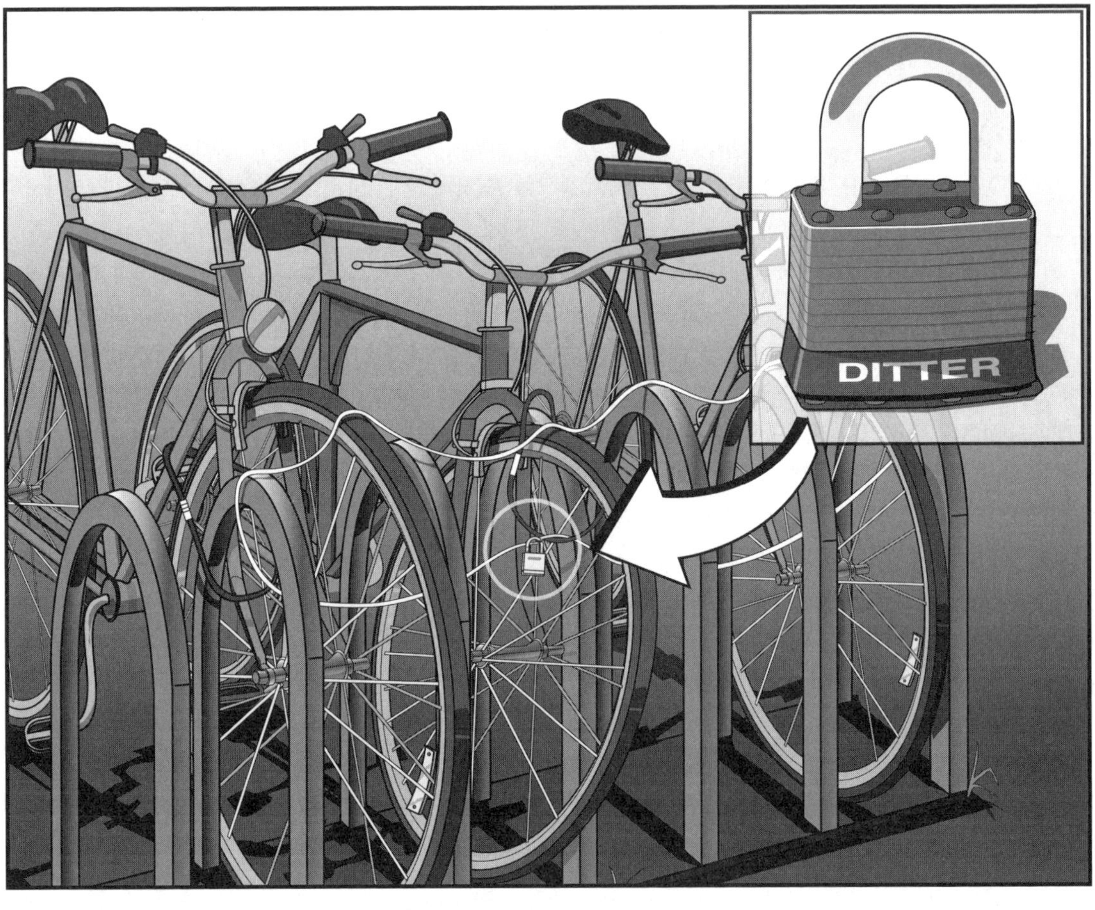

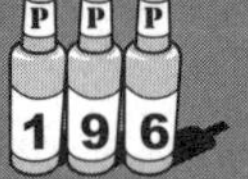

SUCCESSFUL ATTEMPTS																
1	2	3	4	5	6	7	8	9	10	11	12	13	14	15	16	17

WITH ONLY A FEW MINUTES BETWEEN CLASSES, YOU SPRINT OUT OF THE SCIENCE WING AS YOU HEAD TO THE BIKE RACK. YOU PULL ON YOUR P.O.S. (PIECE OF SHIT) BIKE, BUT IT SEEMS TO BE CAUGHT ON SOMETHING. UPON FURTHER INVESTIGATION IT APPEARS THAT SOMEONE HAS LOCKED UP YOUR BIKE. YOUR EYES FOLLOW THE CHAIN AS IT TRAVELS THROUGH SEVERAL OTHER BIKES; YOUR BIKE IS LOCKED WITH ALL OF THEM! YOU KICK YOUR BIKE TIRE AND START HEADING TO YOUR NEXT CLASS, ON FOOT. THIS PRANK WILL COST MONEY—YOU WILL NEED TO PURCHASE OR ACQUIRE A HEAVY-DUTY CHAIN AND LOCK. YOU MIGHT ALSO WANT TO CAPTURE THIS ON CAMERA, WHICH WILL REQUIRE TWO PEOPLE. WORK VIGOROUSLY. YOU MAY ONLY HAVE A FEW MINUTES BEFORE THE NEXT BIKER ARRIVES.

ADDED BONUS: Deflate the bike tires, too. It's quick, simple, and free!

PRANK UNIVERSITY

092 GRAVITY GAMES

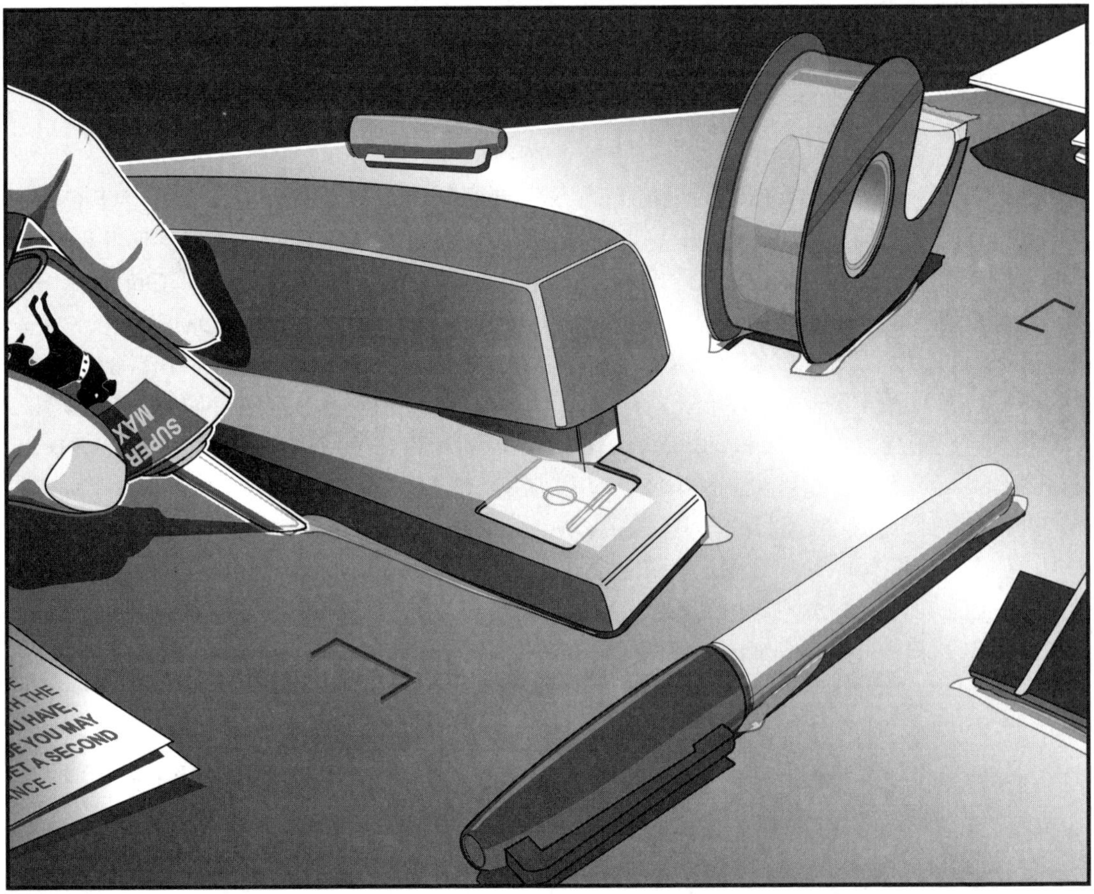

SUCCESSFUL ATTEMPTS

1	2	3	4	5	6	7	8	9	10	11	12	13	14	15	16	17

ARMED WITH A SMALL CONTAINER OF SUPER ADHESIVE, YOU APPROACH YOUR COLLEAGUE'S DESK, LOOKING FOR REVENGE. YOU QUICKLY PICK YOUR TARGETS, AND YOU CAREFULLY BEGIN APPLYING THE GLUE. YOU HIT ALL HIS MAJOR SUPPLIES, SUCH AS HIS TAPE, STAPLER, AND CALCULATOR. THE NEXT TIME HE FINDS THE MOTIVATION TO SIT DOWN AND WORK, HE WILL BE IN FOR A REAL SURPRISE. DEPENDING ON HOW STRONG THAT ADHESIVE IS, HE WILL ONLY BE ABLE TO CALCULATE EQUATIONS, STAPLE PAPERS, OR USE THE TAPE WHILE SITTING AT HIS DESK. THIS PRANK MAY INVOLVE SOME EXPENSES, SUCH AS THE PRICE OF A NEW STAPLER OR CALCULATOR, IF YOU ARE CAUGHT.

ADDED BONUS: "Supply Ball": Glue the items on his desk together to create a huge cluster of desk supplies. You will want to make sure all the items are still usable in order to discourage your colleague from throwing the ball of supplies away.

PRANK UNIVERSITY

093 EARLY SHOWER

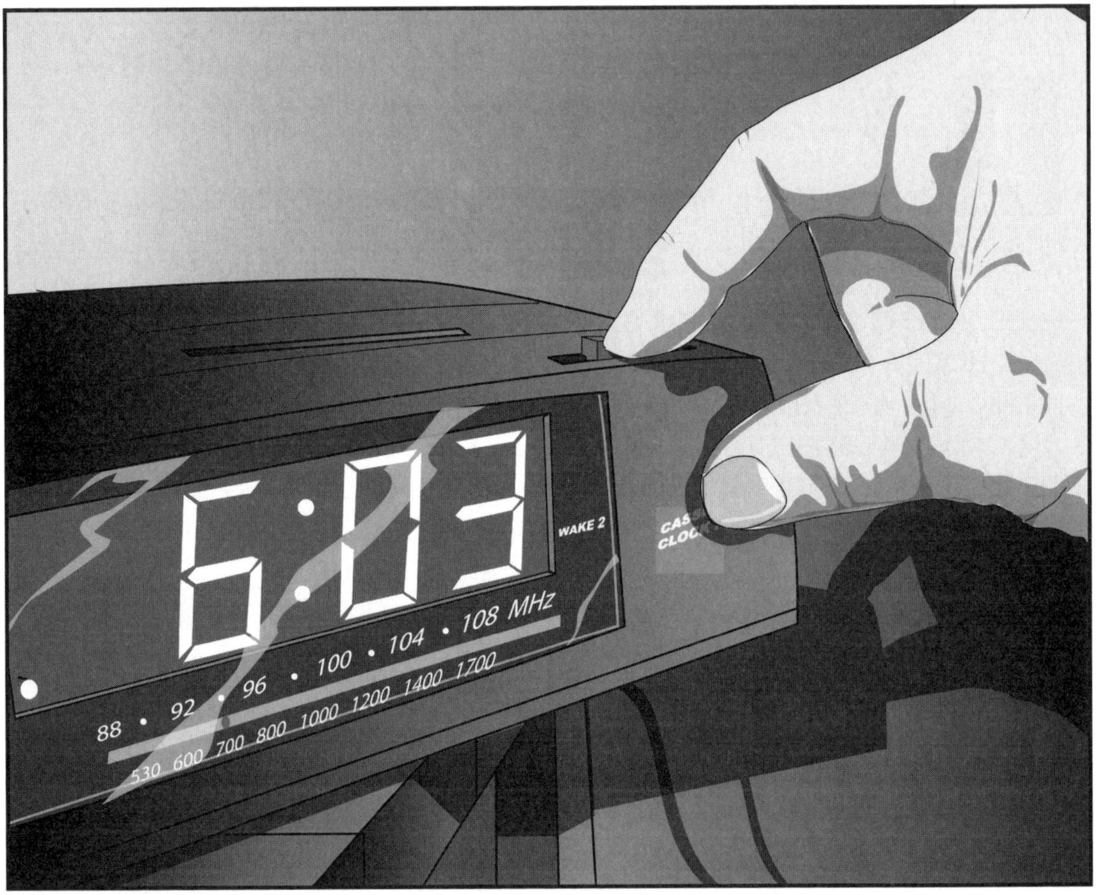

SUCCESSFUL ATTEMPTS

1	2	3	4	5	6	7	8	9	10	11	12	13	14	15	16	17

IT CAME SO QUICK, THE DAWN OF A NEW DAY. THE SUN HAS NOT YET CREPT OVER THE CAMPUS. HE SLOWLY OPENS HIS EYES, ALLOWING THEM TO ADJUST TO THE DARK ROOM. HIS HAND REACHES TOWARD THE ALARM AS HE TURNS OFF THE EAR-PIERCING NOISE. HE BEGINS THIS DAY JUST LIKE EVERY OTHER, WITH A SMALL BREAKFAST FOLLOWED BY A WARM SHOWER. BUT UNBEKNOWNST TO HIM, HIS ROOMMATE HAS ADJUSTED ALL THE CLOCKS IN THEIR APARTMENT. THE EARLY RISER HAS BEEN BAMBOOZLED INTO AN EXTRA-EARLY START TO HIS DAY; HE HAS BEEN FORCED AWAKE ALMOST TWO HOURS EARLY.

ADDED BONUS: Undersleeping is one thing, but oversleeping is another; reset the alarm clock so he sleeps an hour too long.

PRANK UNIVERSITY

094 STICKY SHOWER

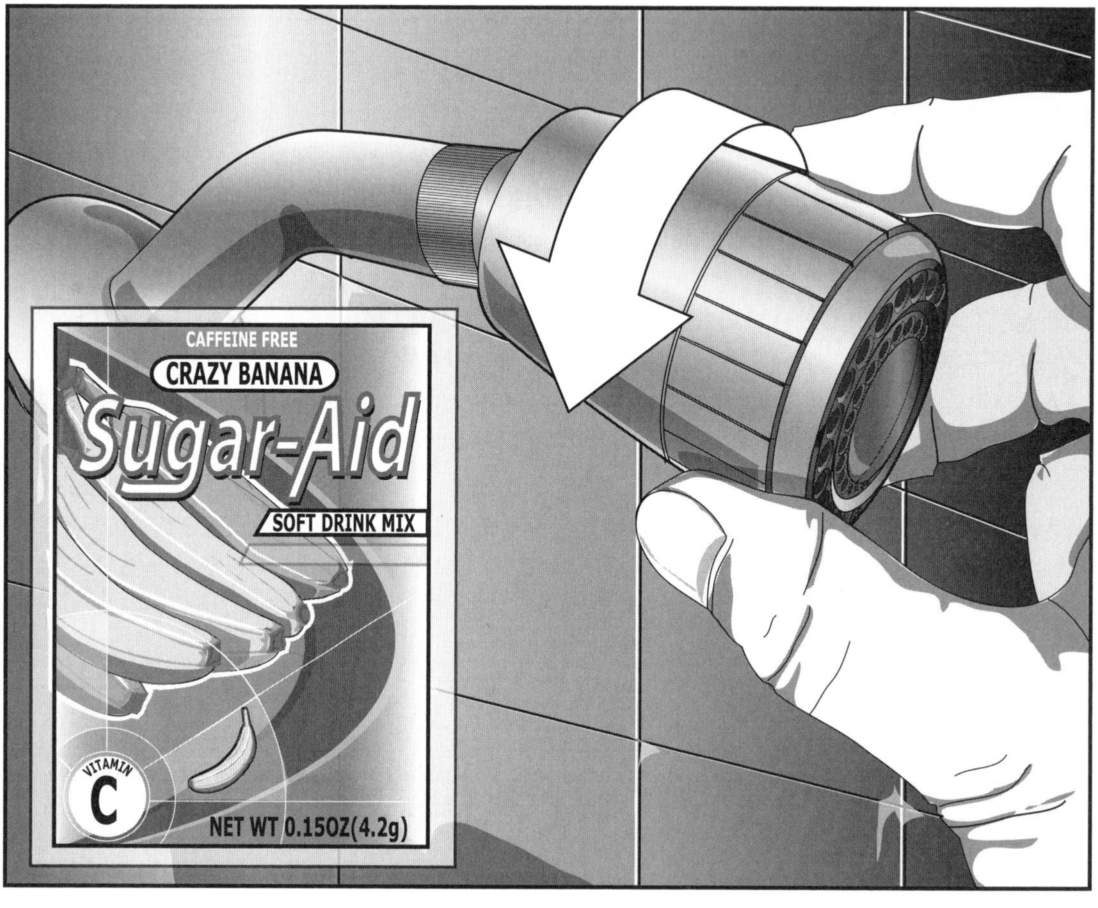

SUCCESSFUL ATTEMPTS																
1	2	3	4	5	6	7	8	9	10	11	12	13	14	15	16	17

DORM SHOWERS ARE DEFINITELY A COLLEGE EXPERIENCE EVERYONE COULD LIVE WITHOUT. IT'S THE ONLY PLACE YOU CAN MEET ANOTHER MAN AND NOT SHAKE HIS HAND AND SAY HELLO. LATE ONE NIGHT, RUN DOWN TO THE DORM SHOWERS WITH KOOL-AID PACKETS OR SOME OTHER BEVERAGE MIX IN HAND. UNSCREW THE SPRAY NOZZLE IN THE SHOWER, AND FILL IT WITH FLAVORED SUGAR. THEN CAREFULLY SCREW THE NOZZLE BACK ON. AFTER A STRENUOUS WORKOUT AT THE GYM, YOUR VICTIM WILL MAKE HIS WAY BACK TO THE DORM TO TAKE A HOT, RELAXING SHOWER. HE'LL GRAB A TOWEL AND HIS FLIP-FLOPS AND HEAD DOWN THE HALLWAY. HE'LL SHOWER FOR SEVERAL MINUTES, AND THEN STEP OUT. LATER THAT DAY HE'LL BE SITTING IN CLASS, TRYING TO FIGURE OUT WHAT SMELLS LIKE WILD BANANA.

ADDED BONUS: Switch the hot and cold knobs. It's quick and simple, but your tired dorm neighbors will fall for it at least a few times.

PRANK UNIVERSITY

095 WET DREAM

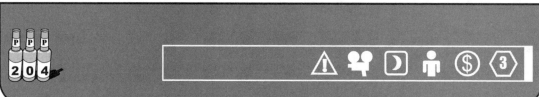

SUCCESSFUL ATTEMPTS																
1	2	3	4	5	6	7	8	9	10	11	12	13	14	15	16	17

IT'S AMAZING HOW MANY CHILDHOOD PRANKS FOLLOW US TO COLLEGE. THIS IS AN ABSOLUTE CLASSIC. YOUR ROOMMATE HAS JUST FINISHED A FUN-FILLED, LIVER-STRESSING NIGHT, AND IT'S INCREDIBLE THAT HE EVEN MADE IT HOME. HE STUMBLES INTO THE HOUSE AND MAKES HIS WAY TO HIS BEDROOM. AFTER A FEW MINUTES, YOU AND YOUR OTHER ROOMMATES BEGIN THE ASSAULT. FILL A BOWL WITH WARM WATER AND SNEAK INTO HIS ROOM. SLOWLY PLACE HIS HAND INTO THE WARM WATER AND WAIT. EVENTUALLY, HE'LL PEE HIS PANTS. IF HE BECOMES TOO STUBBORN TO URINATE, SEE THE BONUS BELOW FOR A QUICK SOLUTION!

ADDED BONUS: Pour water in his lap so he'll wake up thinking he wet his bed. Do this several nights in a row so he thinks he has a bed-wetting problem in addition to his drinking problem.

PRANK UNIVERSITY

096 NO-WHEEL DRIVE

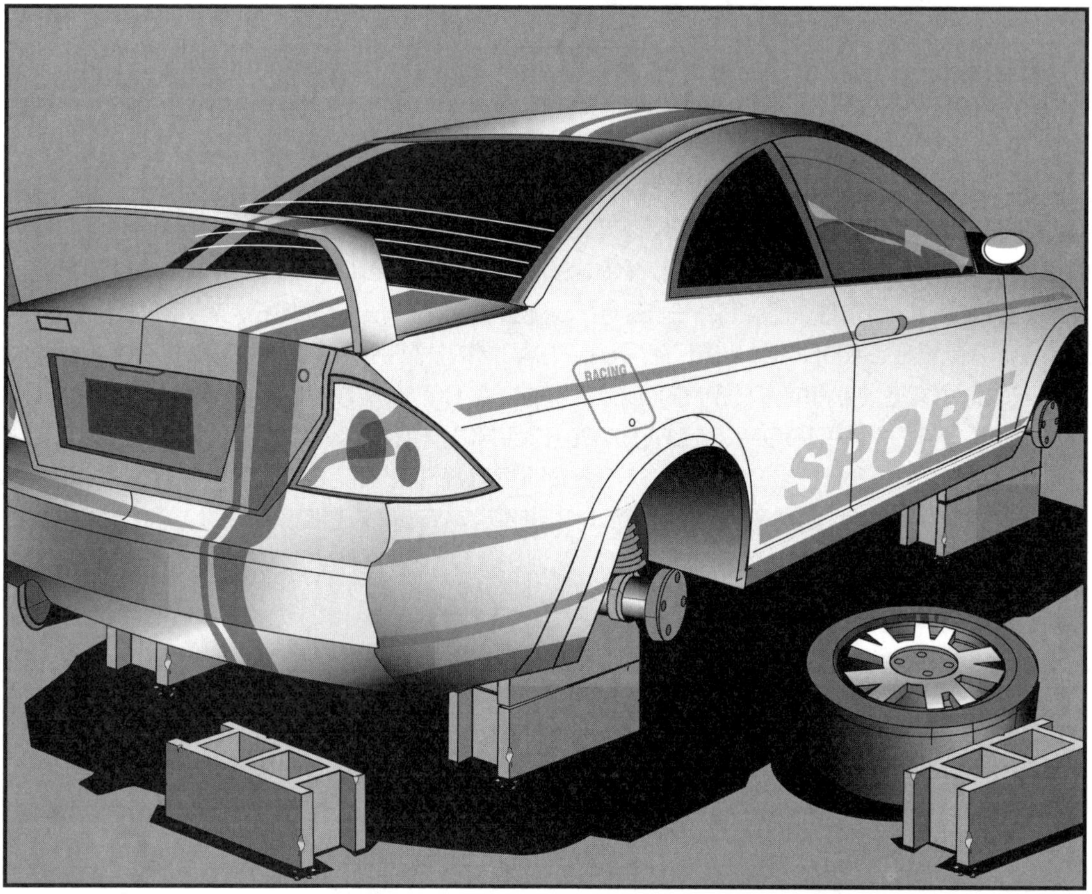

206

SUCCESSFUL ATTEMPTS

1	2	3	4	5	6	7	8	9	10	11	12	13	14	15	16	17

THIS HARMLESS PRANK IS ALSO BORDERLINE CRIMINAL. YOUR BUDDY HAS JUST OBTAINED FOUR NEW NINETEEN-INCH RACING RIMS FOR HIS "RIDE." YOU WILL WANT TO RE-CREATE A CRIME SCENE BY REMOVING THE NEW WHEELS FROM HIS CAR. LATE ONE NIGHT, WITH THE HELP OF YOUR FRIENDS, QUICKLY REMOVE ALL THE RIMS AND DROP THE CAR ON BLOCKS. THEN WAKE THE OWNER OF THE CAR AND TELL HIM SOMETHING HORRIBLE HAS HAPPENED. HE'LL BLOW A GASKET WHEN HE FINDS OUT. IF POSSIBLE, FILM THE WHOLE PRANK. IF SOME DRUNKEN KIDS HAPPEN TO KNOCK THE CAR OFF THE BLOCKS, IT'S PROBABLY BEST IF YOU DON'T FESS UP TO THE PRANK.

ADDED BONUS: You can also put the car on blocks without removing the tires.

PRANK UNIVERSITY

097 POOPY PURSE

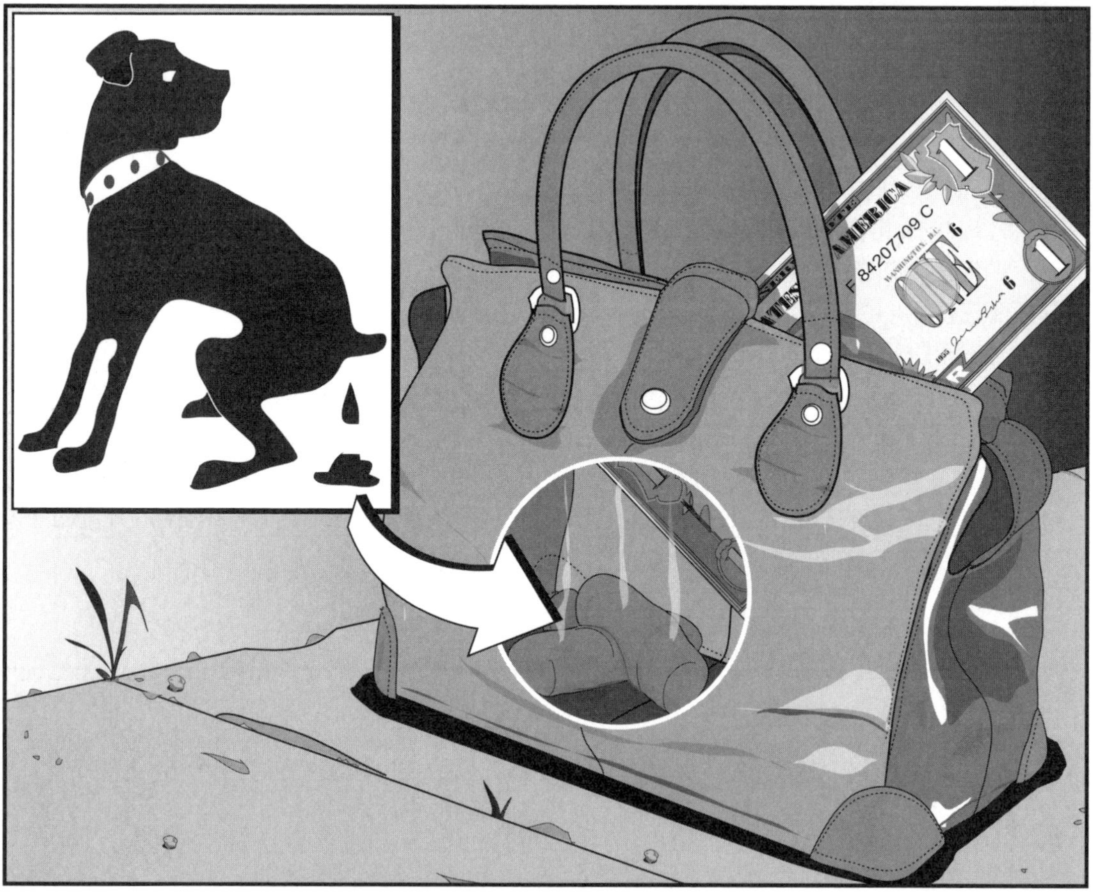

SUCCESSFUL ATTEMPTS

1	2	3	4	5	6	7	8	9	10	11	12	13	14	15	16	17

THE LEAVES FALL SOFTLY ON THE OLD PAVEMENT AS HE TRUDGES DOWN THE STREET, HIS HANDS IN HIS EMPTY POCKETS AS HE SILENTLY CURSES HIS STUDENT LOANS. THEN, IN THE DISTANCE, FINANCIAL OPPORTUNITY: AN OLD LADY'S PURSE, LEFT ON THE SIDEWALK. HE QUICKLY RUNS TO THE PURSE AND NOTICES A DOLLAR STICKING OUT. GREEDY FOR MORE, HIS HAND REACHES IN AND IS GREETED BY FRESH FECES! HIS HAND IS COVERED IN A FUNKY FUDGE BROWNIE. HE DROPS THE PURSE AND RUNS AWAY, AND YOU HAVE THE WHOLE EPISODE ON CAMERA. MAKE SURE YOU PLACE THE PURSE ON A WELL-TRAVELED SIDEWALK, AND BRING PLENTY OF ONE-DOLLAR BILLS SO YOU CAN PULL OFF THIS PRANK A COUPLE OF TIMES.

ADDED BONUS: Tie a string to a dollar bill, hide around the corner, and pull it right when someone is about to grab it.

PRANK UNIVERSITY

098 RAINING MONEY

									SUCCESSFUL ATTEMPTS							
1	2	3	4	5	6	7	8	9	10	11	12	13	14	15	16	17

THIS PRANK WILL COST YOU APPROXIMATELY FOUR DOLLARS' WORTH OF PENNIES. DISPERSE THE COINS ON THE TOP SIDE OF THE CEILING FAN'S BLADES (WHILE IT IS OFF, DUMBASS). YOUR UNWITTING VICTIM WILL FLIP THE FAN SWITCH ON AND BE PELTED WITH PENNIES—HUNDREDS OF THEM. THIS SHENANIGAN IS ONE OF THE MOST HILARIOUS TO WITNESS. IT'S AMAZING HOW FAST ALL THOSE PENNIES COME FLYING OFF, AND HOW THEY END UP EVERYWHERE IN THE ROOM. JUST REMEMBER ONE THING: WE DON'T THROW STONES IN GLASS HOUSES, SO IF YOUR FRIEND HAS A HUGE COLLECTION OF SHOT GLASSES IN HIS OR HER ROOM, I DON'T RECOMMEND THIS PRANK. IF YOU BREAK SOMETHING, REPLACING IT WILL COST YOU A LOT MORE THAN FOUR HUNDRED PENNIES.

ADDED BONUS: You can also place paper cups full of water on the blades. This creates a huge mess and has a ranking of five!

PRANK UNIVERSITY

099 CRIME SCENE

SUCCESSFUL ATTEMPTS																
1	2	3	4	5	6	7	8	9	10	11	12	13	14	15	16	17

DID YOU HEAR THE NEWS? SOME DRUNKEN KID HIT HIS HEAD ON THE FLOOR LAST NIGHT BY THE VENDING MACHINES. I GUESS THE FORENSICS LAB TAPED UP THE SCENE. IT'S CRAZY. GO CHECK IT OUT!" THIS PRANK IS GREAT, BUT IT WILL COST YOU A FEW DOLLARS. YOU WILL HAVE TO RUN TO THE HARDWARE STORE FOR CAUTION TAPE, AND YOU WILL ALSO NEED TO PICK UP WHITE MASKING TAPE TO RECONSTRUCT THE BODY OUTLINE. EARLY ONE MORNING, YOU AND YOUR ROOMMATE MAKE YOUR WAY DOWN TO THE VENDING MACHINES. HAVE HIM LIE ON THE FLOOR, AND TAPE AROUND HIS BODY. YOU MAY WANT TO ADD EXTRA "EVIDENCE," SUCH AS A BOTTLE OF BEER, A LOW-GRADED TEST, A COUPLE OF COINS, OR A DEAR JOHN LETTER. MAKE SURE YOU SPREAD THE WORD!

ADDED BONUS: Fake blood also adds realism, as does convincing a friend to walk past the vending machines every half-hour, pretending to cry.

PRANK UNIVERSITY

100 STRAWBERRY TATTOOS

SUCCESSFUL ATTEMPTS

1	2	3	4	5	6	7	8	9	10	11	12	13	14	15	16	17

YOU ROLL OVER, AND SUNLIGHT HITS YOUR EYES. YOU DECIDE TO WAKE UP, BUT YOU ARE STILL HALF-ASLEEP FROM A LONG NIGHT OF BEER PONG. YOU HAVE TO PEE, SO YOU GET UP AND WALK TO THE DORM BATHROOM. YOU STAND THERE FOR A FEW MINUTES STARING AT USED CHEWING GUM IN THE URINAL. YOU TURN AROUND TO WASH YOUR HANDS, AND THEN IT HITS YOU. THE MAGIC-MARKER MONSTER HAS ATTACKED YOUR FACE. YOUR FRIENDS HAVE MADE YOU A WALKING BILLBOARD, WITH MORE FILTH AND VULGAR LANGUAGE THAN YOU CAN SHAKE A STICK AT. YOU WILL HAVE TO SCRUB FOR HOURS IN ORDER TO REMOVE THE PERMANENT MARKER, RESULTING IN A BRIGHT RED FACE.

ADDED BONUS: Combine this prank with Prank #46, "Sleepy Pedicure," for a good laugh.

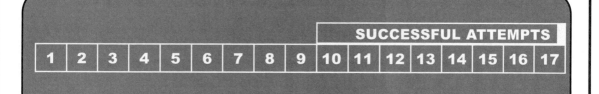

ABOUT THE AUTHOR

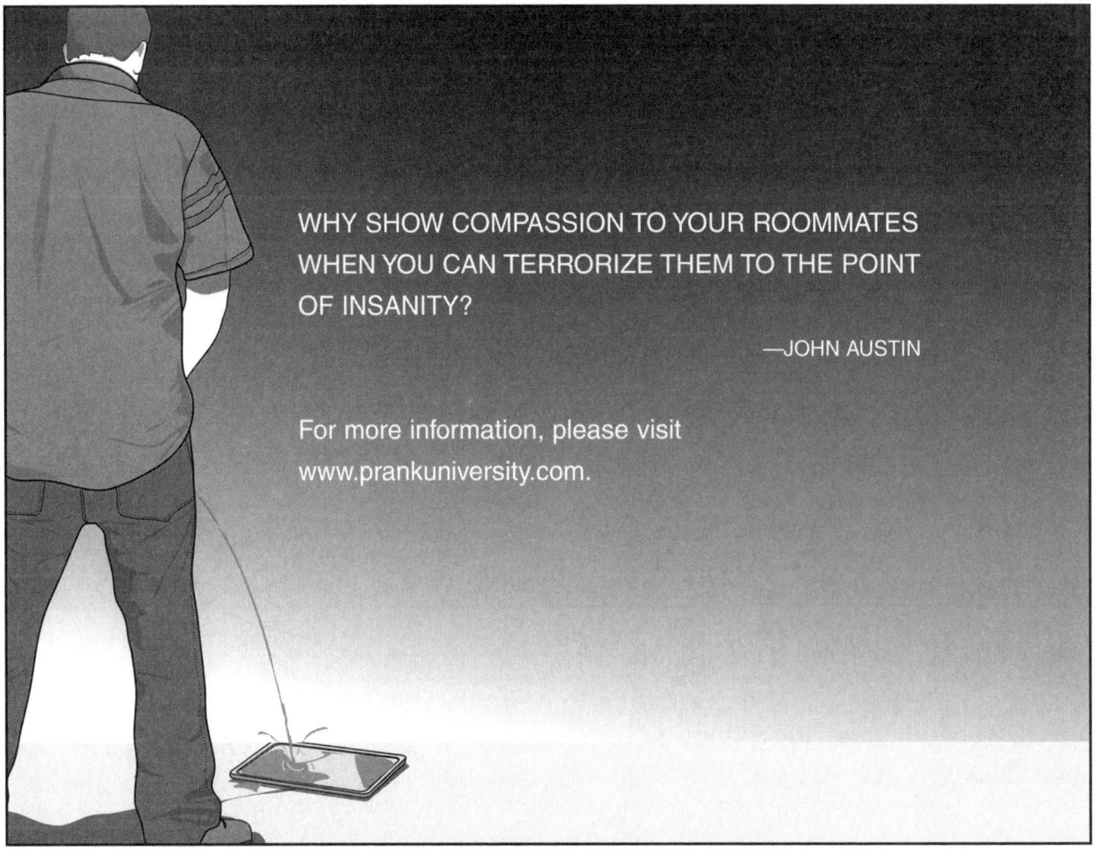

WHY SHOW COMPASSION TO YOUR ROOMMATES WHEN YOU CAN TERRORIZE THEM TO THE POINT OF INSANITY?

—JOHN AUSTIN

For more information, please visit www.prankuniversity.com.

1

PRANK JOURNAL

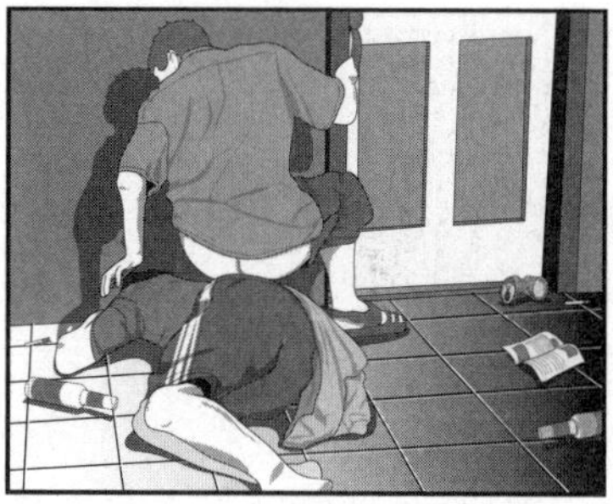

2 PRANK JOURNAL

3

PRANK JOURNAL

4 PRANK JOURNAL

5

PRANK JOURNAL

6 PRANK JOURNAL

7

PRANK JOURNAL